T0194079

Dressed for Church on Sunday Morning

But What about Your Discipleship, Worship, Fellowship, and Stewardship?

Zadia B. Tyson

WESTBOW
PRESS®
A DIVISION OF THOMAS NELSON
& ZONDERVAN

All Scripture quotations, unless otherwise indicated, are taken from the Holy
Bible, New International Version®, NIV®. Copyright ©1973, 1978, 1984, 2011 by
Biblica, Inc.™ Used by permission of Zondervan. All rights reserved worldwide.
www.zondervan.com The "NIV" and "New International Version" are trademarks
registered in the United States Patent and Trademark Office by Biblica, Inc.

Scripture taken from the New King James Version®. Copyright © 1982
by Thomas Nelson. Used by permission. All rights reserved.

WestBow Press books may be ordered through booksellers or by contacting:

WestBow Press
A Division of Thomas Nelson & Zondervan
1663 Liberty Drive
Bloomington, IN 47403
www.westbowpress.com
1 (866) 928-1240

ISBN: 978-1-9736-4093-6 (sc)
ISBN: 978-1-9736-4094-3 (hc)
ISBN: 978-1-9736-4092-9 (e)

Library of Congress Control Number: 2018911529

Print information available on the last page.

WestBow Press rev. date: 12/31/2018

To
George, Beverly, Michael, and Breon; my sisters,
Mae B., Lee Eunice, Louise, Julia Mae, and Daisy;
my brother, Frank; my sister-in-love, Josie;
Nieces, nephews, cousins and friends

My Mount Calvary Baptist church family

And

Sister Celestine Howard and the Christian sisters of
Saint James Baptist Church in Pompano Beach, FL.

Contents

Preface

Growing up in the South in the forties and fifties as an African American child, it was customary for men, women, boys, and girls to have church clothes and shoes. Those clothes were worn to church on Sundays—and Sundays only. All my young life, my mother and Miss Molly (my Sunday school teacher) impressed upon us that church was a special place to be, and for that reason, it was necessary for us to look our best. My fondest memories of church attendance as a child were seasonal. We got all dressed up in our new church clothes and shoes to celebrate Christmas (the birth of our Lord and Savior Jesus Christ) and Easter (His death, burial, and resurrection) in a special church program. We sang songs and recited our individual speeches to honor Him, the gift to us from God the Father to save the world from its sins.

As an adult beginning my Christian journey, I maintained the practice of purchasing and wearing church clothes, because it was a part of my upbringing. Upon becoming a mother, my perception of going to church did not change. I did exactly the same, dressing my children for church, as my mother did for us; they too had church clothes. As a young adult, I must admit that what we looked like when we attended church was probably more important to me than my worship.

In the years to come, my frequent church attendance took on a new meaning. It was during my faithful attendance to church and Sunday school that my perspective of church changed. The change came when I accepted Jesus Christ as my Lord and Savior and a result developed a relationship with Him. One of the best things that ever happened to me was when I was asked to teach the adult Sunday school class. This overhauled my life! I began to study the Bible, and my focus was no longer on what I looked like while attending church but on the grace and mercy of God. I no longer saw church as a place where we gather all dressed up to hear the sermon, read scriptures, and sing songs. I now see church as an important place for my membership and attendance—but more importantly as a nurturing place for my worship, my fellowship, my discipleship, and my stewardship. I must confess that, to this very day, I still have church clothes for Sunday-morning church service. I want to look my best when I go before God to worship and serve Him. That's the kind of reverence I have for Him.

It is my sincere hope that, as you read this book, you too will be enlightened to the fact that your church membership and attendance can become a stepping-stone to the kind of worship, discipleship, fellowship, and stewardship God requires of us, His people.

Unless indicated otherwise, all scripture quotations come from the New International Version of the Holy Bible.

Introduction

Some years ago, I was asked to emcee several "Pretty Hat Tea" church programs at other churches. On these occasions, we all came dressed in our fine church clothes, with matching hats, purses, and shoes of all colors, shapes, and sizes. All the Pretty Hat Tea programs that I participated in were held at churches, and all the ladies were dressed up in their fine church clothes for the occasion. In admiring all the beautiful outfits, I began to wonder where this idea of going to church all dressed up came from. Was it to make us look spiritual in our best outfits or to go before God looking our best? I took the opportunity to search for scriptures that implied that special clothing should be worn when going before God to praise and worship Him during worship services.

In my research, I did find scriptures where the outward appearance was addressed in regard to the temple. In the Old Testament, when God instituted the priesthood, He intended the priest to minister to Him on behalf of the people. He ordered Moses to make holy garments for Aaron and his sons, for glory and for beauty. The outfits consisted of a breastplate, an ephod, a robe, a skillfully woven tunic, a turban, and a sash. They were made of gold, blue, purple, and scarlet thread and fine-woven linen, to be worn before God to minister to Him as priest. Precious stones were set in gold settings, and rings and chains of gold were strategically placed on the garments. Aaron and his sons were to be anointed and consecrated in the holy garments (Exodus 28–29:9 NKJV).

The prophet Elijah wore a garment of hair and a leather belt around his waist. He was called by God to deliver life-changing messages to His people. He challenged them to take a stand and follow God. In the New Testament, God chose someone to do special work for Him—John the Baptist, a distant cousin of Jesus. He grew up in the wilderness, and not much else is known about him until he shows up preaching repentance. He was simply dressed in an outfit made of camel's hair, with a leather belt around his waist. His attire was not meant to be the focus, but rather the message of repentance that he brought to the people. He was the forerunner of Jesus Christ, who came to encourage the people to turn away from sin and to God (Matthew 3:1–6).

Both Elijah and John the Baptist came on the scene with assignments from God for His people. When we look at the attire of these two men, we see that they were certainly dressed differently from everyone else. But what is most important, the clothing or the message? When we look at the appearances of these two prophets, perhaps God wanted them to be able to get the attention of the people so that they could hear from Him. Whatever the intent was, we can conclude that God is more interested in His Word being given to His people, rather than on what the person who is delivering His Word is wearing.

Today, it is common to walk into a church on Sunday morning and see some women dressed in their best outfits, with matching shoes and hats, and men in suits and ties, while others are casually dressed in jeans and a shirt with sneakers or high heels. Their choice of dress does not make them more or less spiritual than anyone else. Coming before God with the proper attitude and conduct in a worship service is more important than what a person is wearing. What they are wearing is not as important as the quality of their worship, their discipleship, their fellowship, and their stewardship, which God requires of all of Christians.

Chapter 1

God in the Lives of Believers

We are who we are because of God the Father, His Son Jesus Christ, and the Holy Spirit that lives in us; all three of the Godhead were present when God said, "Let us make man in our own image and in our likeness" (Genesis 1:26). Being made in His image does not mean we look like Him in human form but that we have an intellect, creativity, desires, and the ability to love and forgive. Throughout the Bible, God's holy Word, He has given us all the instructions and information we need to become the people He desires us to be, so that ultimately we will spend eternal life with Him. God has high expectations of us, His people, but does not ask us to do the impossible. In His Word, He not only tells us what to do, but He also reveals to us how to do it. God wants us to be holy and pursue holy lifestyles. The author of the book of Hebrews wrote that we should make every effort to live in peace with all men and to be holy. Without this, no person shall see God (Hebrews 12:14).

In order to become holy, we must first acquire a personal walk in faith with God the Father, our Creator. This personal relationship with Him comes through fellowshipping with Him through the study of His Word and being obedient to it, as well as through a personal, sincere prayer life. It is a must that we learn of Him, who He is, and who He is to us. Through Jesus Christ and the Holy Spirit that lives in us, all things are possible for us. Scriptures teach us that we can do all things through Christ, who gives us the strength (Philippians 4:13). This includes pursuing a holy and righteous lifestyle. After all, thanks to Adam, we are all born in sin, which makes us sinners.

After receiving our salvation, we must diligently seek to become more like Jesus. This requires studying God's Word to seek holiness and develop a relationship with Him. We must pursue God and His will and way for our lives. Jesus told us how to pursue God when He said that we should ask and it will be given to us, seek and we will find, and knock and the door will be opened to us. Then He assures us that everyone who asks receives; those who seek finds, and those who knock will find the door opened (Matthew 7:7–8). It is those spiritual things of God that He wants us to ask Him for, such as love, understanding, patience, knowledge, compassion, humility, and the ability to forgive. In order for us to grow spiritually and become the disciples that God has called us to become, we can meditate on these words penned by the psalmist. In this wisdom psalm, he said:

> Teach me, O Lord, to follow your statues, then I will keep it to the end. Give me understanding, and I shall keep Your Law and obey it with all my heart.

Make me walk in the path of your commandments, for I delight in it. Turn my heart toward your statues and not toward selfish gain. Turn away my eyes from looking at worthless things, and revive me in Your way.

Establish Your Word unto your servant, who is devoted to fearing you. Turn away my reproach which I dread, for Your judgments are good. How I long for Your precepts! Preserve my life in your righteousness. (Psalm 119:33–40 NKJV)

True worship, discipleship, fellowship, and stewardship are character traits desired by God for His people. As followers of Christ, we must know and live out some basic truths about God that cannot be compromised. We must know without a shadow of doubt that He is who He says He is, and He will do what He says He will do, according to His written Word. We must have faith and trust in God and His Word.

The author of the book of Hebrews says that without faith, it is impossible to please God because anyone who comes to Him must believe He exists (Hebrews 11:6). We must be rooted and grounded in God's principles and doctrines so we can set examples for the new believers in speech, life, love, faith, and purity (1 Timothy 4:12). As we are walking examples, we must live every moment of our lives knowing and teaching these facts about God.

Creator of the Universe

The Bible teaches that God is the Creator of the universe and all that is in it and that He did it in six days. It tells the story of His creations and their order. All that He created came from nothing.

He spoke everything into existence. It began with Him creating heaven and earth on the first day. Everything was dark and void, so He created light.

On the second day, He created the atmosphere to separate the waters from the sky and waters on land.

On the third day, He gathered the waters (oceans, seas, rivers, and more) in one place, and land (the continents) appeared to produce vegetation, including plants bearing seeds according to their kind and trees bearing fruits with seeds in them according to their own kind.

On the fourth day, He created lights to separate day from night and serve as signs to mark days, seasons, and years. The two great lights are the sun to rule the day and the moon to rule the night. He also made the stars.

On the fifth day, He created fish and other living creatures for the sea. They were to reproduce their own kind. On this day, He also created birds to fly above the earth, and they too would reproduce their own kind.

On the sixth day, He created all the different kinds of animals to live on the land. He made each of them to reproduce its own kind. When everything was created and in its proper place, He created man and woman to care for the earth and populate it. As He looked over His creations, He was satisfied that everything He created was good and very good (Genesis 1:1–31 NKJV and NIV).

The Trinity

Although the term *Trinity* is not mentioned in the Bible, God reveals Himself as the Triune God in scriptures, starting with the beginning of time when He said, "Let us make man in our image, in our likeness" (Genesis 1:26). The word "us" is plural; therefore, the words "Let us" signify that there was someone other than Him before the creation of the world. The apostle John began his Gospel by saying, "In the beginning was the Word (Jesus), and the Word was with God, and the Word was God. He was with God in the beginning" (John 1:1–2). We know that the Holy Spirit was also present since the beginning because the Bible says that when God created the heavens and the earth, the earth was formless, empty, and dark, and the Spirit of God hovered over the waters (Genesis 1:2).

In the apostle Paul's farewell blessings to the Corinthian church, he invoked all three members of the Trinity when he said, "May the grace of the Lord Jesus Christ, and the love of God, and the fellowship of the Holy Spirit be with you all" (2 Corinthians 13:14). As he wrote on faith in the Son of God, the apostle John said, "For there are three that bear witness in heaven; the Father, the Word and the Holy Spirit; and these three are one" (1 John 5:7 NKJV). In this one God, all three persons of the Trinity have their individual roles to play in the lives of believers. They are the following:

1. God the Father is sovereign over all that takes place in the universe that He created. He provides the world with what it needs. He is love. He loves humankind so much that He came down to earth in human form to deliver us from our sins so that we can spend eternal life with Him. He is our righteous judge who judges us according to His statutes and commandments. God Himself is the One who will live with us, His people, and be our God forever (Revelation 21:3).

2. Jesus the Son is God in the flesh. He was fully God and fully man. He came down from heaven to save humankind from sin. He died a horrendous death on the cross to fulfill His God-given mission on earth so

that every man, woman, boy, and girl could have eternal life. The apostle John wrote, "For God so loved the world, that He gave His One and only Son, that whosoever believes in Him shall not perish but have eternal life" (John 3:16). He is our Savior and is the only way to God the Father. He is also the mediator between us and God the Father. At present, He is sitting on the right hand of God the Father, interceding for us when we sin and ask for forgiveness.

3. The Holy Spirit who lives in us is the third person of the Trinity. Before Jesus' ascension back to heaven, He promised His disciples that He would send the Holy Spirit to live in them. The Holy Spirit came just as Jesus had promised He would. He appeared on the day of Pentecost to fulfill His divine purpose, which is to lead and guide believers in their Christian walk with God. Being filled with the Holy Spirit, we are no longer controlled by the sinful nature but by the Spirit. We become dead to sin and alive in Christ (Romans 8:9–10).

God's Natural Traits

God is the one and only God and has natural qualities that are attributed to Him and Him only. They cannot be compromised, no matter what anyone says or what we read that is in opposition to what is written in His Word. As children of God, we must believe the following:

He Is Spirit

Jesus said that God is Spirit, and His worshipers must worship Him in Spirit and in truth (John 4:24). He is not a physical being with limitations. He is invisible because He cannot be seen with the naked eye. He has no body or form. And according to the Word of God, He has no beginning and no end. The Bible tells us who He is and what He will do. Because He is Spirit, He can and does make His presence known through His mighty works in nature and in our personal lives.

He Is Changeless

God's character will never change. He is who the Bible says He is since its first writings over two thousand years ago. We live in a changing world, but God remains the same throughout all situations and circumstances. The author of the book of Hebrews said, "He is the same yesterday, today, and tomorrow" (Hebrews 13:8).

He Is Omnipotent

Omnipotence speaks of God being all-powerful. He had the power to create the universe and has the power to sustain it. He can do all things and everything. He is in control of everything that was and is to come. He is the ruler of nature, time, and history. King Solomon wrote, "There is no wisdom, no insight, no plan that can succeed against the Lord" (Proverbs 21:30).

He Is Omnipresent

Omnipresence speaks to the fact that God is everywhere at all times. He is unlimited in His nature. Sitting on His throne in heaven and looking down on earth, He has a bird's-eye view of everything that is going on. The author of Hebrews wrote that nothing in all creation is hidden from God's sight. Everything is uncovered to the eyes of God, to whom we must give account (Hebrews 4:13).

He Is Omniscient

God's omniscience refers to Him having superior knowledge and wisdom and the power to know all things. He has knowledge of the past, present, and the future because He created time. With all His knowing power, He knows everything about people. He knows their thoughts before they are ever spoken, and He knows what they are going to do before they do it. Jesus said of God's omniscience, "And even the very hairs of your head are numbered" (Matthew 10:30).

He Is Eternal

God is eternal in nature. He is the beginning, and there is no end to Him. In John's visions while on the isle of Patmos, God said to him, "I am the Alpha and the Omega, who is, and who was, and who is to come, the Almighty" (Revelation 1:8). He is the eternal ruler over the past, present, and future and therefore sees time in its entirety. The Bible says that when earth and heaven perish, which will be the work of God's hands, He will remain the same, and His years will never end (Hebrews 1:10–11, 12b).

God's Moral Traits

God also has some moral traits that are above all others. There are no flaws in His character, which makes Him perfect in all His ways. As children of God, we cannot compromise these truths but must be able to stand boldly and defend them according to our belief in His Word and our relationship with Him.

He Is Love

God is love, and He showed Himself to be love when He sent His beloved Son to earth to die on the cross for the sins of the world, that we might have eternal life (John 3:16). He is the source of our love, and being created in His image, we must love. John said that anyone who loves has been born of God, and anyone who does not love does not know God, because God Himself is love (1 John 4:7–8).

He Is Grace

God's grace is a free gift to humankind. It is the favor God shows to us when we do not deserve what He give to us. It cannot be earned but is voluntarily given to those He saves. His grace is for everyone, and without it, nobody can be saved from their sins (Ephesians 1:6–7).

He Is Holy

God is a God of love, mercy, and grace. He is perfect, righteous, and pure. His holiness and righteousness refers to His moral excellence. He has set high moral standards for us, His people, and He calls us to be holy because He is holy (1 Peter 1:15–16). Although God loves us unconditionally, it is because of His holiness that He cannot contend with sin in the lives of His people.

He Is Faithful

Faithfulness is one of God's key attributes. There is no failure in Him. Whatever He says He will do, He will do just that. He will remain faithful to us even when we are not faithful to Him. He will keep His promises and fulfill His Word because He cannot disown Himself (2 Timothy 2:13).

He Is Merciful

God shows His mercy when He helps those of us who do not deserve His help because of our sinfulness. The psalmist wrote, "He does not treat us as our sins deserve or repay us according to our iniquities" (Psalm 103:10).

He Is Righteous

The righteousness of God refers to the moral laws He gave to guide the conduct of humankind. His righteousness is always the same. He affirms what is right and rejects what is wrong. He cannot and does not contend with sin. He is righteous in all His ways and loving toward all He has made (Psalm 145:17).

He Forgives

Forgiveness is the act of excusing someone for their wrongdoings. God's love for humankind causes Him to forgive sinners and accept them as His own. No sin is so bad that it cannot be forgiven. When He forgives us, He does not count it against us anymore (Psalm 32:2). It is God's nature to forgive us, His people, for our sins, and because He forgives us, He expects us to forgive those who treat us wrongly.

He Is Good

God's goodness consists of righteousness, holiness, justice, kindness, grace, mercy, and love, which clearly makes Him the source of all goodness. The psalm writer said to God, "You are good, and what you do is good" (Psalm 119:68a). When Jesus was called "Good teacher," He said, "No one is good but One, that is God" (Mark 10:18 NKJV).

He Is Truth

God acts in truth and speaks in truth. He is true to humankind and true to His Word. Anything or anyone else we put our trust in can fail us, but His Word will stand forever (1 Peter 1:25). Moses said that our God is a God that cannot lie or change His mind (Numbers 23:19a).

God in His infinite wisdom set the stage for His people to be able to play out their God-given roles of discipleship, worship, fellowship, and stewardship when, through Jesus Christ, He gave us His church which was founded upon the death, resurrection, and the ascension of Jesus Christ back to heaven. Without these important events, there would be no church.

Chapter 2

The Church

The concept of "the church" began with some questions Jesus had for His disciples. He asked them who the people thought He was. They answered that some said He was John the Baptist or one of the other prophets. Then Jesus asked them, "Who do you say that I am?" Simon Peter, one of His disciples, revealed His identity when he said, "You are the Christ, the Son of the Living God." Jesus told him that he was blessed and that humankind did not reveal that to him, but the Father in heaven did. Then Jesus said, "Peter, on this rock I will build my church, and the gates of Hades will not overcome it." The rock on which Jesus would build His church has been identified as Jesus Himself and His work of salvation by dying on the cross for the sins of the world, and with Peter, the first leader in the church of Jerusalem (Matthew 16:16–18). Paul added to this by teaching that the church was built on the foundation of the spiritual things taught by the apostles and prophets, with Christ Jesus Himself as the chief cornerstone. It is in Him that the building is joined together and rises to become a holy temple in the Lord (Ephesians 2:19–21).

Paul taught that the church is subject to Christ because Jesus gave Himself up for the church to make it holy and blameless. There could not and would not be the church without the shedding of Jesus Christ's blood for the sins of humankind, His resurrection, and His position at the right hand of Father God in heaven. God placed all things under His feet and appointed Him to be head over everything for the church (Ephesians 1:20–22).

Its Origin

The church was established in Jerusalem on the day of Pentecost. Pentecost was a Jewish festival that was celebrated fifty days after Passover. Jewish people from all over the world came to Jerusalem to celebrate in the festival. On Jesus' last days on earth, He told His disciples to remain in Jerusalem and wait for the promised gift of the Holy Spirit. This would be the fulfillment of what John the Baptist spoke of when he told the people that One more powerful than he would come and baptize them with the Holy Spirit and with fire (Luke 3:16). The Holy Spirit came fifty days after Jesus' resurrection and ascension to heaven. The small group of eleven men had grown to over 120 followers of Jesus Christ. The apostles were gathered in one place, and they were there on one accord when the presence of the Holy Spirit came. Luke said, "There came a sound from heaven as of a rushing mighty wind, and filled the whole house." Next, "they saw what appeared to be tongues of fire that separated and came to rest on each of them. All of them were filled with the Holy Spirit, and began to speak with other tongues (unknown languages) as the Spirit enabled them." When the God-fearing Jews from every nation heard the apostles speaking to them in their native languages, they were bewildered, and because they did not understand what was happening, they accused the disciples of having too much to drink (Acts 2:1–13).

The apostle Peter addressed the crowd and defended the behavior of the disciples by saying that the disciples were not drunk, as it was only nine o'clock in the morning. But this is what was spoken by the prophet Joel when he said, "And it shall come to pass in the last days, says God, that I will pour out My Spirit on all people" (Acts 2:15–17a). Peter, empowered by the Holy Spirit, preached boldly to them about Jesus Christ, whom he said was sent by God, and they, with the help of wicked men, nailed Him to the cross. After His death, He was resurrected from the dead by God. After hearing Peter's message, they were cut to the heart and said to Peter and the other apostles, "Brothers, what shall we do?" Peter answered, "Repent and be baptized, every one of you, in the name of Jesus Christ for the forgiveness of your sins. And you will receive the gift of the Holy Spirit," (Acts 2:22–38).

Many of the listeners accepted Peter's message and were baptized, and about three thousand people were added to the number of believers and to the community of faith. These new Christians devoted themselves to the apostles' teachings, to the fellowship, and to the breaking of bread and prayers. They had all things in common. Many of them sold their possessions and goods and divided them among those who were in need. They continued daily with one accord in the temple, and they broke bread from house to house and ate their food together with gladness and simplistic hearts, praising God and enjoying each other. And the Lord added to their numbers daily those who were being saved (Acts 2:40–47 NKJV).

The Universal Church

The word "church" has more than one meaning. The first reference is to the universal church, which has a worldwide membership, with Jesus being the head of those who follow Him (Colossians 1:18a). The universal church is in the heart of the believer. It is the spiritual family of believers in Christ. There is no physical assembling of the members, but they are all joined in this church by their faith in Jesus Christ. They do not meet in a building, but they follow Jesus Christ regardless of time and place. They are joined together by their belief in the birth, death, and resurrection of Jesus Christ, which makes them members of God's household and citizens in His kingdom. We can say the church is the people who believe in and follow Jesus Christ. When Paul wrote to the church of Ephesus, he listed seven beliefs of the universal church, which unites all Christians. They are:

> *One body*: all believers are a part of this body.

> *One Spirit*: that is the Holy Spirit who dwells in both the church and in the individual believer.

> *One hope*: believing we will have an eternal home with God one day.

> *One Lord*: that is Jesus Christ, who is head of the church.

> *One faith*: our belief that binds us together in Him and is the only faith that is required for salvation.

> *One baptism*: it is most likely the baptism of the Holy Spirit, which is the placing of each of

us into His body (vs. 5, *Nelson's Compact Bible Commentary*).

One God and Father: of all, above all and through all, and in us all (Ephesians 4:4–6).

Most of the first believers in Jesus Christ were Jewish people. Because of their rejection of Jesus Christ and at God's appointed time, the apostle Paul presented God and His plan for salvation to the Gentiles. This posed a problem between the Jews and Gentiles because the Jewish people could not accept the fact that God was offering salvation to the Gentiles (Acts 13:46–48; 18:6). When the Gentiles became believers in Jesus Christ, Paul informed them that they now had the same access to Jesus as the Jews, because they were now part of the body of Christ, the universal church. He told them that they were no longer foreigners and aliens but were fellow citizens with God's people and members of God's household, which is built on the foundations of the apostles and prophets, with Jesus Christ as the chief cornerstone. He said it is in Jesus Christ that the whole building is joined together and rises to become a holy temple in the Lord. It is in Him you too are being built, to become a dwelling in which God lives by His Spirit (Ephesians 2:19–22).

The Local Church

The second reference is to the local church. This church refers to a building where believers assemble to worship and praise God. This church is God's spiritual house, where Jesus is the head. It is comprised of a group of baptized believers who meet in buildings (some are edifices, some are traditional church houses with steeples, and some are storefronts) to worship and praise God and to be instructed in His Word. The first church was manifested in Jerusalem. It consisted of believers who met for communion, prayer, and teachings about God and His Word (Acts 2:46–47). The apostle Peter portrays the church as a living, spiritual house, with Christ as the foundation and cornerstone, and each believer as a stone (1 Peter 2:4–8). God's house, the church, is one of prayer, praise, and help. Believers attend church to worship God and develop a closer relationship with Him. This is done through praise and worship, prayer, hearing His Word, seeking to experience His presence, serving Him and others, and fellowship with other brothers and sisters in Christ. As a result of the Holy Spirit living within the believer, they develop a personal relationship with God the Father. The believer now belongs to the community of faith, and church attendance becomes an important part of their life, rather than just being a part of their lifestyle.

The early Christians did not keep the Jewish Sabbath but set aside the first day of the week, Sunday, as the Lord's Day, a day for rest and worship. It was observed on the first day of the week because that was the day Jesus Christ was resurrected from the dead. They understood there could be no church without the death, resurrection, and ascension of the Lord Jesus Christ. Since the beginning of the church, the Lord's Day has been kept holy. Christians still meet on Sunday, the first day of the week, in buildings designated for the preaching of God's Word, prayer, worshiping, praising Him, and experiencing His presence.

Purpose

The purpose of the church is to reveal Jesus Christ to the world. This is done by proclaiming the Gospel of Jesus Christ to reach lost souls. It is to teach people to have faith in the one and only true God. The church is also to nurture, encourage, and provide for each member spiritually so that they can live a life of faith. God's people are called to worship Him. Jesus said, "God is Spirit, and His worshipers must worship Him in spirit and in truth" (John 4:23–24).

The church is commissioned to make disciples, so they can know how God wants them to live and not just get people saved to become church members. Therefore, our worship services must be conducted in an orderly and godly manner so that the worshipers can get to experience God in a personal way, empty themselves before a holy God, and then know that they have been in the presence of the Lord on that day.

One Body

The apostle Paul refers to the church as the "body of Christ." He says the church is one unit that has many members. The many members make up the one body. He compares the church to the human body, which is made up of many different individual parts. Each member of the church and each part of the human body has a purpose, and they have different functions but must work together. Comparing the church to the human body was his way of showing the importance of members of the church working together while still performing individual duties. Each person is needed with his or her gift in order for the church to serve its purpose as Jesus called it to do, just as each part of the body is needed for the body to function properly.

Paul said that the human body is a unit made up of many parts and each part is important and has a role to play in order for the body to function properly. As examples, he used the foot, the hand, the eye, and the ear to show that if these small parts are missing or cannot perform their natural duty, the body becomes unable to function as a whole, because some seemingly less important parts are missing (1 Corinthians 12:12–29). This same principle applies to the church with its many members. If the body of Christ had all prophets and teachers and none of the other gifts that God gave to equip the church, it would be a dysfunctional church. All the gifts that God gave to the church are needed to help meet the needs of the body of Christ and to respond to the call God has on the individual lives in the church.

Unity

The church is built on one foundation, and that is Jesus Christ. Unity in the church speaks of brothers and sisters united in Christ, who is the head of the church. The apostle Paul wrote to the Roman church, "So in Christ, we who are many form one body and each member belongs to all the others"(Romans 12:5). This does not mean that people will not have different opinions, but he taught the believers that they should agree with one another so that there will be no divisions among them; then they will be perfectly united in mind and thought to do the work of Christ (1 Corinthians 1:10). Christians must speak out for what is right and true, but it has to be done in a loving, kind way. The Holy Spirit creates unity in the church because it is necessary to carry out God's plans for His church. He encourages each member of the church to be committed to doing their part to help the church become what God has called it to be.

Unity is important in the church because there is joy in being able to work together in harmony. There is no place in the church for discord. With dissensions in the midst of church, we cannot do the work of Christ. David said it was good and pleasant when brothers live together in unity

(Psalm 133:1). Discord causes our focus to be on ourselves and not on Christ. Unity enables us to work together as a body that is able to agree to disagree. The one thing the church cannot disagree on is its purpose.

Paul said that we are to live a life worthy of the calling we have received from God. This is referring to our behavior and demeanor in the church, as well as our character. He gave four characteristics of the children of God that will form the foundation in them for the unity God wants His people to have in His church.

The first one is to be humble. It promotes harmony in us. The second one is to be gentle. We are to be kind to one another, fair and compassionate. The next one is to be patient. When we see faults in others, we must be able to bear with them in love. The last one is to keep peace. This is done when we make God our focus and not ourselves (Ephesians 4:1–3).

Spiritual Gifts

Spiritual gifts are God-given abilities given to every member of the body of Christ to empower them for service to the Lord and His body, the church. The apostle Peter said that each one should use whatever gift they have received to serve others (1 Peter 4:10). Paul explained that while there are different kinds of gifts, "service and working," they all come from God. God knows us, His people, so He gives each of us the right gifts so that we may serve Him and others in the ways He wants it done. All Christians have at least one spiritual gift, but some have more than one, and all of them are given according to the will of the Holy Spirit (1 Corinthians 12:4–11). These gifts are given by the Holy Spirit so that the ministries they produce may glorify God. The work should be done as an act of praise to God, and the attitude and quality of the work should honor Him. All gifts are from God, and they all have the same purpose—that is, to benefit the whole church. In order for these God-given gifts to be used effectively, as God desires, they must be practiced with love (1 Corinthians 13, 14).

The apostle Paul introduced a list of gifts in the letters he wrote to the churches in Rome, Corinth, and Ephesus. The apostle Peter also spoke of gifts in his first letter to the Jewish Christians. One gift alone can't do the work of the church, but all the gifts working together can make God's church grow and function effectively. Paul said that God gives gifts to build up the church, and it is the duty of each member to seek ways to serve others and God with the gift that He has given them. He said the gifts were given "for the equipping of the saints for the work of ministry, for the edifying the body of Christ" (Ephesians 4:12 NKJV).

These are some of the gifts (not all) found in the church that the apostles Paul and Peter wrote about. Some of these gifts are more prominent than others, and some seem to be performed behind the scenes, but God sees them all as equally important to the church. They are:

> **Administration** (1 Corinthians 12:28): The gift of administration is the God-given ability to understand the goals and purposes of a particular ministry of the church, then organize and execute effective plans for the supervising of others in order for the goals to be accomplished.

> **Apostleship** (1 Corinthians 12:28; Ephesians 4:11): The gift of apostleship is the God-given ability to assume and exercise general leadership over a

number of churches and maintain authority in spiritual matters of those churches.

Different Kinds of Tongues (1 Corinthians 12:10, 28; 14:13–19): The gift of different kinds of tongues is the God-given ability to speak to God in an unknown language, or to speak in an ecstatic language that could not normally be understood by the speaker or the hearers.

Distinguishing between Spirits (1 Corinthians 12:10): The gift of distinguishing between spirits is the God-given ability to recognize God's truth from false information, by being sure certain behaviors said to be of God are really of God and not of Satan.

Encouragement (Romans 12:8): The gift of encouragement is the God-given ability to offer words of encouragement, comfort, and consolation, to counsel others in crisis, and to help them be all that God has called them to be.

Evangelism (Ephesians 4:11) The gift of evangelism is the God-given ability to spread the good news of Jesus Christ to unbelievers as well as believers. They travel from place to place, preaching the Gospel, seeking to lead people to Jesus Christ.

Faith (1 Corinthians 12:9): The gift of faith is the God-given ability to display confidence in God, His power, and His promises, being so confident in Him that no matter what happens, circumstances and obstacles do not shake their conviction.

Giving (Romans 12:8): The gift of giving is the God-given ability to joyfully share with others what material resources one might have, without expecting anything in return.

Healing (1 Corinthians 12:9): The gift of healing is the God-given ability to be used to serve as a human mediator through whom God cures illnesses and restores health, not of a natural means.

Helper (1 Corinthians 12:28): The gift of being a helper is the God-given ability to willingly and systematically give support and assistance to others in the ministry, so as to free them up for ministry.

Hospitality (1 Peter 4:9–10): The gift of hospitality is the God-given ability to warmly welcome people, even strangers, into one's home or church as a means of serving and meeting their needs.

Interpretation of Tongues (1 Corinthians 12:10, 14:27–28): The gift of interpretation of tongues is the God-given ability to translate a message that is spoken in unknown tongues.

Knowledge (1 Corinthians 12:8): The gift of knowledge is the God-given ability to seek to learn as much about the Bible as possible, then share the information with others for the spiritual growth and maturity of the body of Christ.

Leadership (Romans 12:8): The gift of leadership is the God-given ability to set goals in accordance with God's purpose for the future of the church and communicate these goals to others in such a way that they will be motivated to get involved and work harmoniously to accomplish those goals.

Mercy (Romans 12:8): The gift of mercy is the God-given ability to show kindness, give comfort, and be sympathetic to those who are suffering due to circumstances beyond their control. But more importantly, it is about meeting their needs with deeds of love to help rid them of their pain and suffering.

Miraculous Powers (1 Corinthians 12:10): The gift of miraculous powers is the God-given ability to serve as a human mediator of God to perform powerful acts that are acknowledged to be supernatural.

Pastor (Ephesians 4:11): The gift of being a pastor is the God-given ability to spiritually lead and guide a group of believers entrusted in one's care.

Prophecy (Romans 12:6, NKJV; 1 Corinthians 12:10): The gift of prophecy is the God-given ability to receive and communicate an immediate message of God to His people. (This gift was especially valuable to the church before the scriptures were completed.)

Service (Romans 12:7): The gift of service is the God-given ability to identify the unmet needs involved in a task related to God's work and to make use of available resources to meet those needs.

Teaching (Romans 12:7; 1 Corinthians 12:8; Ephesians 4:11): The gift of teaching is the God-given ability to communicate information relevant to Christ to other members in such a way that they may learn and grow in Christ.

Wisdom (1 Corinthians 12:8): The gift of wisdom is the God-given ability to understand and apply knowledge to life situations so that God's spiritual truths can come alive and be applied daily when problem-solving.

After the apostle Paul gave His lists of spiritual gifts to the various churches and to us, he told the people in the church of Corinth that the greatest gift given to humankind and the church is love. Love gives credence to all the other gifts. Being concerned that some spiritual gifts in the church were not being used properly, he wrote that whatever gift one might have, it is nothing if it is not done with love. Love is the greatest of all gifts, and while some are temporary, love will last forever (1 Corinthians 13:1–13).

Dress Code

The way a person dresses to go to church is no indication that they are more or less spiritual or holier than anyone else in the church. We all know that looks can be deceiving. Jesus warned His disciples about people's outward appearances that seem to make them appear righteous. The religious leaders walked around in flowing robes, which gave them the appearance of holiness, and they loved to have the best seats in the synagogues. They were hypocritical because behind their appearance of holiness, they oppressed the widows, who the Old Testament prophets and New Testaments apostles insisted they care for (Exodus 22:22–23; James 1:27). They presented themselves to be holy and righteous, but they were not obedient to God's Word. Jesus said they would be punished more severely because of their hypocrisy (Mark 12:38–40).

A person's choice of dress for church is a personal decision. The only thing we can conclude is that what someone wears does tell something about them: it can indicate whether someone is liberal or conservative in their thinking; it sometimes tells what a person can afford; and it could be that they are aware that God does not have a dress code for church services, so they come as they are. Some people dress up, some dress down, and some *just dress* for church, but hopefully what they all have in common is that they go to church for a praise and worship experience. Throughout the ages, people have been noted for how they dress, whether it is rich and fancy or poor with no frills. In today's society, people tend to be more accepted when they are well dressed in the church and in other places as well. The apostle Paul addressed the issue of what women should wear to church when he gave some instructions on worship. His position was that he wanted their focus to be on Christlike character rather than looking beautiful. Every time the Bible refers to "clothing oneself," or "putting on," it is in regard to one's spiritual life and not to the outward appearance.

The Word of God is specific in what Christians should be clothed in and what we should put on. Once we have accepted Jesus Christ as our Lord and Savior, our conduct changes to match our new faith. The apostle Paul said that we should take off the old self with its practices and put on the new self, which is being renewed in knowledge in the image of God (Colossians 3:10). As we change, we are to become more like Him spiritually. In both the Old and New Testaments, scriptures address what we are to put on or clothe ourselves in; and in each scripture, it refers to the righteousness and holiness of God.

We do see in scriptures that God gave Moses instructions on what the priests should wear. After traveling through the desert and reaching the foot of Mount Sinai, God gave the Ten Commandments and instructions for how to build the temple. He also instituted the priesthood in order to teach the people how to serve Him. In doing so, He told Moses to make special garments for Aaron, the first priest, and his sons, who were to become priests. These garments were made from blue, purple, and scarlet yarn and fine linens. The priests wore a beautiful outfit to the tabernacle each day. Their garments were to be sacred and used for ministering in the sanctuary (Exodus 28; 39:1–31).

In the book of Numbers, the Lord commanded the people of Israel to make tassels on the corner of their garments, with a blue cord on each tassel. This was a reminder that they were to remember all the commands of God so that they could obey them and not go after the lusts of their own hearts and eyes (Numbers 15:37–39).

Job was a man of faith and patience, and God allowed him

to go through much suffering, both mentally and physically. He lost all of his children and possessions, his body was covered with sores, and his friends doubted him. They told him that his condition was due to sin in his life. Job did not agree with their cause for his predicament, but he did not have the answer either. He did not understand why he was suffering, because he knew he was a servant of God. God said of Job to Satan, "There is no one on earth like him; he is blameless and upright, a man who fears God and shuns evil" (Job 1:8). Throughout his whole ordeal, he did not feel like he deserved what he was going through. Through it all, Job still acknowledged God as "Almighty God." Just before God restored everything back to Job, He told him to adorn himself with glory and splendor and clothe himself in honor and majesty (Job 40:10). Job was to get ready for what God was about to do in his life.

In the book of Isaiah, he addressed "to be clothed" on several occasions. In chapter 3, God made mention of some women of Judah who were self-centered. Their focus was not on Him but on clothing and jewelry. They cared nothing about the needs of the poor people around them. This displeased God, and He promised that the day would come when He would snatch away all of their fancy clothes and jewelry (Isaiah 3:16–26). Also, in chapter 52, Isaiah offered the exiles words of comfort, as they would be restored to their homeland. He told them to wake up and clothe themselves with strength. They were to put on their beautiful garments, for the uncircumcised and unclean (the enemy) would no longer come to them (Isaiah 52:1 NKJV).

Again the prophet Isaiah proclaimed the Word of God to the Israelites. He gave them hope after calling them to repent of their sins. He wrote, "I delight greatly in the Lord; my soul rejoices in my God. For He has clothed me with garments of salvation and arrayed me in a robe of righteousness, as a bridegroom adorns his head like a priest, and as a bride adorns herself with her jewels." He was speaking about his new glorified condition in the Lord (Isaiah 61:10).

In one of the prophet Zechariah's visions, he saw Joshua, the high priest, standing before the Lord and Satan in filthy clothes. The high priest represented the people before God and in no way should have been defiled. The Lord had Joshua's filthy clothes removed and clothed him in rich, clean garments. Joshua's filthy clothes represented sin, and his rich, clean garments represented the righteousness and holiness of God (Zechariah 3:1–4).

In the New Testament, in the book of Romans, the apostle Paul had the opportunity to teach about being a good citizen in the kingdom of God. There were some things he said that we must not do, and some things we must do in our relationships with God and other people. He told his listeners that the first thing they had to do was to love their neighbor as they loved themselves, realizing that love does not harm one's neighbors. His message to them was that they had to make a change. They had to stop doing the ungodly things they were doing during the night hours and put on daytime behaviors at all times. He told them that the hour had come for them to wake up from their sleep, because salvation was closer than they first believed. He told them to put aside the deeds of darkness and put on the armor of light. They should behave decently, as in the daytime, not in orgies and drunkenness, not in sexual immorality and debauchery, not in dissensions and jealousy. Rather, they should clothe themselves with the Lord Jesus Christ and not think about how to gratify the desires of the sinful nature (Romans 13:9–14).

In the Corinthian church, there were different nations of believing women in the same church. They were in a cultural disagreement as to whether they had to have their heads covered during public worship services. It was such a serious issue that it was dividing the church, and this was a grave concern of the apostle Paul, the founder of that church. It was cultural for the Jewish women to cover their heads, whereas the Gentile women thought it was not necessary to have their heads covered during worship services. To resolve the issue and create unity in the church, Paul explained God's sovereignty in creating the rules for relationships. He said that the head of every man is Christ, and the head of every woman is man, and the head of Christ is God. He said that every man who prays or prophesies should not cover his head but that every woman who prays or prophesies should cover her head to honor her head, the man whom she was created for, and God is his head. He said it is also because of the angels who were obviously present in the meetings that the woman ought to have a sign of authority on her head. After his explanation, he told them to make the judgment call if it was proper for a woman to pray to God (her Creator) with her head uncovered (1 Corinthians 11:3–13).

Timothy was a young church leader who was given instructions by the apostle Paul. Paul had sent Timothy to the church at Ephesus to address some false teachings that the church was dealing with. In these verses, he particularly addressed and hoped to resolve the issues of how the Christian women dressed within the church. After observing their behavior in regard to this matter, he apparently came to the conclusion that the women were trying to gain respect by their outward appearances rather than by becoming Christ like in character. Paul wanted them to know that their outward appearances were not nearly as important as their inner beauty. He told them that he wanted the women to dress modestly, with decency and propriety, not with braided hair or gold or pearls or expensive clothes—rather with good deeds, as this was appropriate for women who professed to worship God

(1 Timothy 2:9–10). He was not telling the women that they should not make themselves look attractive, but he did want them to know that beauty begins on the inside and that a loving Christian character cannot be duplicated by the wearing of cosmetics and jewelry.

In his letters to the churches of Rome, Galatia, Ephesus, and Colossae, Paul informed the members that they needed to change their ways. He used the analogy of changing clothes. Believers in Christ have to take off the old ways and put on new ways. The old clothes represent sinful ways and are not suitable for the new convert. The change to new clothes represents putting on God's righteousness. Therefore, he gave them a list of things they had to take off; some of them were orgies, drunkenness, sexual immorality, debauchery, dissension, and jealousy. Since Paul told them what they needed to take off, he also told them to put on the things of God and His righteousness, to clothe themselves with the Lord Jesus Christ and not to think about how to gratify the desires of the sinful nature (Romans 13:14; Galatians 3:27).

He said to the church of Ephesus that they should be made new in the attitude of their minds, put on the new self, created to be like God in true righteousness and holiness (Ephesians 4:23–24). As Christians, the old life before Christ is dead; therefore, the believer puts on a new self with a new way of thinking and living because of the Holy Spirit that lives in him.

Paul also taught that believers are new creatures in Christ and that the old ways of the sinner should not be the ways of the believer, who is now filled with God's Holy Spirit. In his letter to the church of Colossae, he gave them a list of old practices that they had to get rid of, everything that belonged to their earthly nature. He told them that since they had taken off their old selves with those practices, they needed to put on their new selves with new thoughts and practices. These are not "good ideas" that Christians get, then make plans to implement them; instead, they are traits that guide their attitudes and actions toward others who are saved or unsaved. He referred to them as God's chosen people, holy and dearly loved, as he told them how to get dressed. He said:

> Clothe yourselves with compassion, kindness, humility, gentleness and patience. Bear with each other and forgive whatever grievance you may have against one another, Forgive as the Lord forgave. And over all these virtues, put on love, which binds them all together in perfect unity. (Colossians 3:5–14)

Paul wrote about what God wants us, as Christians, to be clothed in. They are clothes of righteousness that are an outflow of the Holy Spirit living in the believer. They are:

Compassion: To be clothed in compassion is not to feel sorrow for someone but to actively help those who are in need due to circumstances beyond their control.

Kindness: To be clothed in kindness is having the ability to consistently show compassion to others, as opposed to judging them for the situation they are in.

Humility: To be clothed in humility is being able to exalt and praise someone else, especially Jesus Christ, and not think too highly of oneself, putting others first while maintaining a good attitude about oneself.

Gentleness: To be clothed in gentleness is to be able to be kind, polite, generous, and courteous when interacting with all people.

Patience: To be clothed in patience is to be able to endure the shortcomings of others without their being aware of it.

Forgiveness: To be clothed in forgiveness is a requirement by God to let go of resentment for a wrong that has been committed toward you.

Love: To be clothed in love is to be able to love others as we love ourselves; being able to be merciful and compassionate to anyone who is in need, regardless of who it might be. This kind of love meets the needs of others, without expecting anything in return (Colossians 3:12–14).

There is an ongoing struggle that is forever present in the life of the Christian. The two forces that are in constant battle within are the Holy Spirit and the sinful nature that humankind was born with. The Holy Spirit's job is to lead and guide God's people according to His doctrines and His way. Satan's job is just the opposite. He tries to sway God's people away from Him by deception and other means. He and his angels are real; although they can't be physically seen, they are alive and well. They are the enemies of God. They are powerful and are constantly trying to entice God's people to come over to their side. The spiritual enemy is stronger than we are in the natural, but the

Holy Spirit that lives in us gives us the needed power to stand up to the devil. We must be able to put up a good fight with no intention of losing when we are in battle with the devil.

Paul said that in order for us to win this battle, we must first of all be strong in the Lord and in His mighty power; that is, we must know who we are in Christ Jesus. He said that when we put on the whole armor of God, we will be able to take a stand against the devil's schemes. He did not say *if* the day comes; instead, he said *when* the day comes, we will be able to stand our ground. It is important to be clothed spiritually because he said that our struggles are not against flesh and blood but against the rulers, authorities, and powers of this dark world and against the spiritual forces of evil in the heavenly realm. We need the power of God through the Holy Spirit to fight against Satan and his angels. Paul said we should clothe ourselves in "the whole armor of God," not just parts of it, but all of it. The expression "armor of God" symbolizes the equipment that we as Christians need for protection when we enter into battle with Satan. They are the resources that God has made available to us, His followers, in order for us to be victorious in our fight with Satan over and over again (Ephesians 6:10–17). To be spiritually ready to go into battle against Satan, he said we should put on:

> **The Belt of Truth**: To put on the belt of truth refers to the integrity of the believer who must be truthful and honest. When we can be honest with God and ourselves, we can be honest with others.

> **The Breastplate of Righteousness**: To put on the breastplate of righteousness refers to the righteous character and deeds of believers.

The Feet Covering of the Gospel of Peace: To have the feet covering of the Gospel of peace refers to the believer's feet always being ready to go out and spread the Gospel.

The Shield of Faith: To put on the shield of faith refers to the believer having faith in the Lord God Almighty. Nothing will change about what we know about our God.

The Helmet of Salvation: To put on the helmet of salvation refers to the believer knowing that they are saved from sin and that they belong to the family of God no matter what Satan says.

The Sword of the Spirit: The sword of the spirit is the only offensive weapon in the believer's armor. To put it on refers to using God's holy and righteous Word in all situations.

James, the brother of Jesus, wrote that Christians should not show favoritism based on a person's outward appearance. He said if a man comes into a meeting wearing a gold ring and fine clothes, and another comes in wearing shabby clothing, the man who is dressed well tends to be treated better than the man who is dressed poorly. God does not approve of such behavior and wanted them to know that He loves everyone and is looking at the heart and not the outward appearance. James addressed this situation by saying:

Have you not discriminated among yourselves and become judges with evil thoughts. Listen my dear brother: Has not God chosen those who are

poor in the eyes of the world to be rich in faith
and to inherit the kingdom He promised those
who love Him? (James 2:1-5)

The apostle Peter wrote about the behavior of the Christian women who had unsaved husbands. He instructed them not to make their outward appearance their main focus, but instead let their godly behavior excel over all else. He was not telling them not to make themselves beautiful, but he did want them to know that developing their inner character and becoming more like Jesus Christ was more pleasing to God than their outward appearances. And to be godly was the way to win their husbands to the acceptance of Jesus Christ as their Savior. He told them that the wives should be submissive to their husbands, so that if any of them did not believe the Word, they might be won over without words, but by the behavior of their wives. When the husbands saw the purity and reverence of their lives, their beauty should not come from outward adornment, such as braided hair and the wearing of gold jewelry and fine clothes. Instead, it should be that of their inner selves, the unfading beauty of a gentle and quiet spirit, which is of great worth in God's sight. For this is the way the holy women of the past who put their hope in God used to make themselves beautiful (1 Peter 3:1–5).

A person's outward appearance has no spiritual value. According to the apostles who addressed this subject matter, they taught that God is only interested in how we should dress ourselves spiritually. That is, He is looking at our godly characteristics. How we dress, whether up or down, to attend church on Sunday morning is not nearly as important to God as having a clean heart to come into His presence to worship Him and serve others. He favors no one but loves everyone equally. He looks at the heart and not the outward appearance.

Chapter 3

Discipleship

True Christian discipleship is a committed pledge to the service of God despite the other demands of life. So, to define a disciple, we must say he or she is a person who has made a total commitment to willingly follow Jesus Christ and His teachings by putting everything else aside. The Christian puts Jesus Christ first in his or her life. This is done out of love for Jesus Christ and not a sense of duty. God did not call us just to be saved but to become disciples. We become His disciples when we pattern our lives after Him by giving up all that we are to become like Him. A true disciple is loyal to Jesus Christ above everything and anyone else. Jesus made His standards for discipleship known when He told the great multitude that followed after Him that if anyone who comes to Him does not hate their father and mother, wife and children, brothers and sisters, and yes, even their own life, they cannot be His disciple. He added that anyone who does not carry their cross and follow after Him cannot be His disciple (Luke 14:26–27). This can only happen by the power of the Holy Spirit that lives in the believer. Only then will we be able to deny ourselves of those things that we thought were important to us, giving up our selfish ways and surrendering our lives to Him.

According to the Bible, discipleship is required of all believers in Christ. We know this to be true because Jesus gave His disciples what we call today "the Great Commission" for making other disciples. He told His disciples to go and make disciples of all nations. They were to baptize them in the name of the Father, the Son, and the Holy Spirit. They were to teach them to obey everything He taught them, and He promised them that He would be with them always (Matthew 28:19–20). Not only did Jesus tell His disciples to go and make other disciples, He told them how to do it. Obviously, they must first have accepted Jesus Christ as their Lord and Savior, because Jesus said to baptize them. Baptism is an outward showing to the world that they are now in the family of God and have repented of their sins. Next, He said to teach them to obey everything He commanded. He knew teaching was important because, before beginning His ministry here on earth, He chose twelve men called disciples to follow Him. These men were from all walks of life, and none of them had any significant leadership abilities or high levels of education. Five of them were fishermen, one was a tax collector, and the occupations of the other six disciples are unknown. However, they did have one thing in common, and that was the willingness to follow Jesus after He said, "Follow Me!" Because of their backgrounds and former teachings, Jesus had to teach them God's principles and statues in order for them to be equipped to carry out His work after His ascension back to heaven. They also had to understand that following Him would be a new life for them and that they could expect to be rejected by many because of their choice to follow Him.

Jesus called His disciples to be salt and light in a world filled with wicked and evilness. Both of these make a significant difference in our world today in more ways than one. Salt brings out the flavor in foods and has the ability to preserve and heal. Light shines and therefore can be seen in darkness. As Christians, we are called by Jesus Christ to make a difference in this world. When He said we are the salt of the earth, He was telling us that we must affect the lives of people in positive ways. He then said we are the light of the world. In this dark world, Christians should glow like lights in darkness to show others the way to Jesus Christ. Jesus said that we should let our lights shine before men, that they may see our good works and glorify our Father in heaven (Matthew 5:13–16 NKJV).

As we grow in Christ, our actions reflect personal knowledge of Him. We walk in His truths and live lives of holiness. The world must be able to see God in us as we live in this sinful world. It is true, we are in this world, but we are not of this world. We are holy and set aside for kingdom building. As disciples of God, we possess character traits that separate us from the world. We must have the traits that follow below.

Living Faith

Faith is the foundation of our relationship with God. We walk in faith every day of our lives. We begin our day in faith that God is with us and is going to provide, protect, and keep us. The author of the book of Hebrews said, "Faith is being sure of what we hope for and certain of what we do not see" (Hebrews 11:1). Faith begins with hearing God's Word, then studying to understand it, being able to acknowledge that God does indeed exist, is indeed who He says He is, and will do what He says He will do, and then finally believing in what He has already done. It is only then that we are able to have faith in Him. Christians should hope and strive to have mountain-moving faith, the kind of faith Jesus told His disciples about as they displayed such little faith when they could not heal a demon-possessed boy. Jesus told them if they had faith as small as a mustard seed, they would be able to say to the mountain, "Move from here to there," and remain steadfast to see it move. Then He added, "Nothing will be impossible for you!" (Matthew 17:14–21). This gives us the right to believe that we can do all things through Christ who gives us the strength (Philippians 4:13).

The author of the book of Hebrews dedicated a whole chapter with examples of Bible characters who demonstrated their faith in God while in unpleasant situations; in fact, there did not seem to be a way out in many cases. These are all examples of how people lived by faith. All these people were still living by faith when they died. They did not receive the things promised, but they continued to have faith in God. They put their faith to work and did what they were called to do in spite of their circumstances and not realizing what the end would be (Hebrews 11:4–39). They did it, and so must we!

In the book of James, he said faith without works is dead, and according to him, faith and actions go together. He said that true faith transforms us. It changes our conduct as well as our thoughts. This is represented by our actions and not on our recitation of scriptures or praying long prayers. One way to test it is to see if our actions change to works. If they do not, then we don't truly believe the truths that we say we do (James 2:14–22). Our faith is made complete by what we do and not what we say. Someone coined the phrase, "Much faith, much power; little faith, little power; no faith, no power." There is some truth to this statement because there are many who have received their salvation and are at a standstill in their Christian lives. The apostle Paul refers to them as "babes in Christ" because they are immature in their spiritual lives and have not moved from salvation to begin the process of sanctification. They have not allowed themselves to work on developing faith in God. Just believing that God exists is not enough. It requires faith in Him to study His Word and learn of Him so that we are able to step out and do what He has called us to do. There is power in knowing and trusting God's words.

Epitome of Love

God is love and is the source of love. Because He is love and we are His people, He demands that we too must love. In order to love others, we must love Him first with all our hearts, minds, and strength, and then love our neighbors as we love ourselves. The apostle Paul wrote that we should be imitators of God and live a life of love (Ephesians 5:1–2a). We too must show love to everyone, just as He did. The apostle John wrote in his first letter about God's love and ours. He said that we should love one another, for love comes from God, and whoever does not love does not know God, because He is love. Then he said whoever lives in love lives in God, and God in him (1 John 4:7–8, 16b).

Love is the key to Christian living and is empowered by the Holy Spirit. It is the greatest of all human qualities. It involves unselfish service rendered to others, showing that one cares. As Christians, we are indebted to love one another. Just as we continually meet our own needs, we are indebted to meet the needs of others. The Bible says that loving one another is a debt that we will never pay off. Paul wrote that we are to let no debt remain outstanding, except the continuing debt to love one another. He said that those who can love their fellow man have fulfilled the law (Roman 13:8). It may seem like Jesus took it to an extreme when He taught that we should love our enemies, do good to those who hate us, bless those who curse us, and pray for those who mistreat us, but this is the kind of love that God has for us and therefore expects of us (Luke 6:27–28). Love is ever present, especially when we are able to be there for others in spite of what is going on in our lives. This kind of love can only be exhibited by those who have accepted Jesus Christ as Lord and Savior and the Holy Spirit who lives in us. This is what the apostle Paul said about the nature of true godly love:

> Love is patient, love is kind, It does not envy, it does not boast, it is not proud. It is not rude, it is not self-seeking, it is not easily angered, it keeps no record of wrongs. Love does not delight in evil but rejoices with the truth. It always protects, always trusts, always hopes, and always perseveres. Love never fails. (1 Corinthians 13:4–8a)

Love shows itself in actions, not in feelings. The greatest act of love in the history of the world was when Jesus Christ died on the cross for the sins of the world. That was a sacrificial act of love for all humankind. Love begins in the heart and then extends itself naturally at the appropriate time. To show love is not a choice; it is commanded by God that we love. There are different kinds of love, but God commands us to love others as He loves. Agape love is the kind of love God commands His people to have for one another. It's not the kind of love we have for special people in our lives, but is shown to anyone who is in need. This kind of love expects nothing in return, and has no limitations. Love is not what we say but what we do from the heart. It shows up in the form of kindness, compassion, consideration, faithfulness, and gentleness toward others. The apostle John said in his letter that we should not love with words or tongue but with actions and in truth (1 John 3:18).

According to Paul, the gift of love is superior to all other gifts. It is a Christian virtue and a requirement for all Christians. We are identified as Christians by the love we show to others.

Student/Teacher

Before we can teach, we must first be students. As Christians, we must learn of God—who He is and how He wants us to live. Then we will be able to teach others. Being able to transfer wisdom, understanding, and knowledge is a characteristic of a disciple. Teaching has a great impact on the lives of people because words and examples affect the lives of people either positively or negatively. In the spirit world, the effects must be positive. James wrote that being a teacher of God's Word carries an awesome responsibility and that the teacher should be held accountable for what is being taught. He said those who teach will be judged more strictly. God's Word is truth and cannot be compromised to suit lifestyles or purposes. Jesus was a teacher of scriptures during His earthly ministry. He taught and trained His disciples so that they would be equipped to spread the Gospel. The same holds true for us today as His disciples. If we are to teach and train others, as is required of us, we must first diligently study and meditate on God's Word. As disciples of God, we must be well versed in scriptures so that we are able to recognize erroneous teachings and dispel them by pointing out that which is of God and that which is not of God. The Holy Spirit, as our teacher, will reveal to us what we need to know, as it is imperative that we have the proper understanding of scriptures so we can teach the whole truth of God and His Word. The Holy Spirit will teach us and also remind us of things we have been taught (John 14:26). Then as disciples of God, we must live in obedience to the Word and teach it to others who are called to become disciples of God and not just members of a church.

God created us in His own image. Therefore, there are many intelligent people on this earth who have worked hard to earn secular degrees. But intelligence and secular degrees do not make us disciples of God. We must know the Word of God, abide in it, and spread it. Someone came up with biblical terms for letters of earned degrees and transposed them to refer to the work in the kingdom of God. These degrees in biblical terms were put on tote bags to sell to Christians who wanted to make a statement about who and what we believe in. One of my friends gave me one, and I carry it proudly while out in the mission field. The first one given to us is our BA degree—born again. The next is our BS degree—baptized and sanctified. As we continue on our Christian journey, the next degree is our MBA—my belief affirmed. Finally, we claim our PhD—praise Him daily. These degrees represent our spiritual growth from the day we accept Jesus Christ as our Lord and Savior until we are what is referred to as "mature Christians in Christ Jesus." All born-again Christians have the right to claim these Christian degrees as we study and apply God's holy Word to our daily lives. Then we can be about our Father's business of helping others to learn of God and His principles and doctrines.

Servant

In the body of Christ, there is room for every Christian to serve. It is God's will that we serve one another. He gives the gift to serve, then gives us the mind to serve in that capacity with dignity and pride. Paul mentions specific gifts of leadership, including apostles, prophets, evangelists, and pastor-teachers. The primary role of these gifts is to help others exercise their gifts to be prepared to serve so that the body of Christ may be built up (Ephesians 4:11–12). Jesus' ministry was one of servitude, and on this Christian journey, we must consider ourselves as servants of the Lord. We must give of ourselves in order to serve Him. Paul said that in our service, we must serve wholeheartedly, as if we were serving the Lord and not humankind. One way to show love is to serve. One of the best examples of servanthood and humility given in the Bible is when Jesus bent on His knees to wash the feet of His disciples. He told them that He did not come to be served but to serve (John 13:4–5).

True humility is the first step in being able to make a true commitment to serve others. The apostle Paul said we should have the same attitude as Jesus Christ, and that is one of humility. Jesus was the perfect picture of humility, giving up His home in heaven in order to come to earth to die a horrendous death on the cross so that His people could have eternal life. As Christians, Paul said that we must realistically be able to see ourselves as God's humble servants. We must be able to evaluate ourselves and truly know that we do not think of ourselves more highly than we ought; rather, we think of ourselves with sober judgment, in accordance with the measure of faith God has given to us. He also said we should not be proud but be willing to associate with people of low position, and we must not be conceited (Romans 12:3, 16). He also taught that we should do nothing out of selfish ambition or vain conceit, but in humility, we should consider others better than ourselves. And each of us should look not only to our own interests but also to the interests of others (Philippians 2:3–4). He said we are to give of ourselves daily. The apostle Peter wrote that each of us should use whatever gift or gifts God has given to us to serve others (1 Peter 4:10). The apostle Paul tells us to present our bodies as a living sacrifice, holy and acceptable to God, which is our reasonable service (Romans 12:1 NKJV).

We serve because we are called by God to serve. Our willingness to obey God's Word and to serve others become real when sacrifices are made to help others and nothing is expected in return. The opportunity to serve is always present as we come in contact with others on a daily basis. Serving is an act of showing God that we love and obey Him. When we serve others, this does not make us their servants but shows that we love them. When we reach that stage in our Christian life, we become ready to serve without an invitation to do so.

Now more than ever before, the opportunity presents itself for helping others outside the church. We should never be too busy or feel too important to help anyone, regardless of our differences. As Christians representing God, whenever we see a need and can help, we don't wait to be asked; we just do it. This is what Jesus did in His ministry here on earth. He helped those who needed help, both physically and spiritually, no matter who they were. Our services rendered to others should be done in a way that honors the call God has upon our lives as His disciples.

In order that Jesus' disciples might understand how God responds to faithful servanthood while waiting for His return, He told the parable of the master who went away and left his servants with talents according to their abilities, to be used in his absence. Two of the servants were faithful; they worked and multiplied the talents they had been given. Upon the master's return, he said to the two, "Well done, good and faithful servants! You have been faithful with a few things; I will put you in charge of many things. Come and share your master's happiness." The third man, who was obviously lazy and received nothing for doing nothing, was cast out (Matthew 25:14–28). Although God is going to reward us for the service that we render, this is not the real reason we serve. We serve because it is an integral part of our discipleship (Ephesians 6:7). Serving God by serving others will prepare us to be servants to God in the New Jerusalem (Revelations 22:3b).

Prayer Warrior

The most powerful connection a Christian can have with God is through prayer. Prayer is communication between God and us. There is spiritual value in praying both individually and collectively. There is a time and a place for group prayers, but it is very important that we spend time alone in prayer with God. As disciples of Christ, we must have persistent, personal prayer lives. When we pray, we open our minds and hearts to give and receive from Him. The apostle John said that we should have confidence in approaching God. If we ask anything according to His will, He hears us. And if we know that He hears us, whatever we ask, we know that we have what we asked of Him (1 John 5:14–15). We realize that He is the Almighty God who is our Creator and loves us. We pray about all issues of life, knowing that He hears us, and we wait for His answers. He will do things for us that we cannot do for ourselves, and so in humility, we go to Him in prayer, knowing that He already knows what's going on with us but is pleased that we can acknowledge that we need Him. The Bible tells us to pray continually and give thanks in all circumstances, for this is God's will for us (1 Thessalonians 5:17–18). Therefore, we can pray any time and all the time, no matter where we are or what we are doing. God hears short, meaningful prayers as well as lengthy ones, whether spoken loudly, softly, or silently. As we pray, we too must pray by faith. Prayers that are offered by faith have to do with the faith of the one who is offering the prayer. Scripture tells us that the prayers of the righteous are powerful and effective (James 5:13–16).

Consistent prayer is so very important in the life of the Christian. So much so, that I believe it is the only way for us to begin and end our day and that we should pray during the day as well. It's a welcome opportunity to open up to Him, telling Him what's on our minds and in our hearts and preparing ourselves to hear from Him. When we tell God about our problems, ask Him to bless others, give thanks to Him, or just offer praises to Him for His goodness, we display our faith and trust in Him. We pray because we need Him. As efficient as we think and hope we are, we need our Father God in heaven. There are times when we must fast and pray. Praying and fasting are spiritual disciplines that bring us into a closer relationship with God as we focus on Him and His goodness.

Jesus Christ the Savior was without sin, yet He found a need to spend time alone praying to God, telling Him what was on His heart. Since He found a need to pray, surely we—as imperfect people who depend on Him for our every need to be met—must pray. The apostle Paul gave four instructions on how we should pray. First, he said we should "pray in the spirit on all occasions, and keep on praying." These can be prayers of praise, supplication, forgiveness, spiritual strength, and more. Next, he said we should "pray with all kinds of prayers and request," meaning we are to pray different kinds of prayers and requests, without regard to the circumstances. Third, he said we are to "be alert," meaning to be aware of needs that must be met. Lastly, he said we should "pray for all the saints," meaning we are to pray for all our sisters and brothers in Christ worldwide (Ephesians 6:18). Since we are required to pray for one another, one of the things we should pray for, among others, is their spiritual growth, as Paul did when he prayed for the Colossian church. He asked God to help them to know what He wanted them to do; to give them deep spiritual understanding; to help them live for Him; to give them more knowledge of Himself; to give them strength for endurance and to fill them with joy, strength, and thankfulness. He said he prayed this prayer for them in order that they might live lives worthy of the Lord and please Him in every way, bearing fruit in every good work (Colossians 1:9–11).

As believers, we should not only pray for our brothers and sisters in Christ but also pray for nonbelievers. It is our Christian duty to pray for them. We don't know why they have not accepted Jesus Christ as their Lord and Savior, and that gives us all the more reason to pray for them. It is through our prayers that they might be saved. God saved us, and they too can be saved. In Paul's instructions to Timothy on worship, Paul urges us to pray for everyone. He said that it pleases God our Savior, who wants all people to be saved and to come to the knowledge of the truth (1 Timothy 2:4). We should pray for them that they will come to their senses and escape the trap of the devil, who has taken them captive to do his will (2 Timothy 2:26).

Our formal prayer time should be a humbling experience, where we allow God to increase, and we decrease because of who He is. When we as Christians go before the throne of grace and mercy in prayer, God expects us to be in obedience to His will and His way when we come to Him with our requests. Jesus said, "If you abide in Me, and My Words abide in you, you will ask what you desire, and it shall be done for you" (John 15:7 NKJV). Psalm 23 also teaches us that we can pray with confidence, knowing who God is and that He will not deprive us of anything, as He is our Good Shepherd. David, the psalmist, made it clear from his experiences with God that he knew he could count on God to meet all of his needs, whatever they were. We, like David, must put all our faith and trust in God and be obedient to His Word. As a result, when we pray, we expect Him to answer our prayers. God is always ready to answer our prayers when we have repented of our sins.

Jesus taught that we must watch and pray so that we will not fall into temptation. He added that the spirit is willing, but the flesh is weak. We cannot put our flesh under control. It only comes through the Holy Spirit that lives within us (Mark 14:38). We should devote ourselves to prayer and wait on God to answer, knowing that He answers prayers. Jesus assures us that when we pray, our prayers will be answered, but that we must ask "in the name of Jesus" (John 14:13–14). God does not always answer our prayers in the way we want them answered, but He does answer. Sometimes the answer is "Yes," sometimes it is "No," and sometimes it is "Wait." But whatever the answer is, we know that God knows what's best for us. There are various types of prayers that, as Christians, we are moved to pray, and we pray them all by faith:

> **Prayers of Confession**: As Christians, we still sin and fall short of the glory of God. The apostle John wrote that if we claim to be without sin, we are deceiving ourselves and the truth is not in us. Therefore, when we sin, we ask for forgiveness, and he said God is faithful and just and will

forgive us our sins (1 John 1:8–9). Being able to acknowledge our sins to Him brings us closer to God because there is now nothing standing between Him and us.

Intercessory Prayer: Christians go before God on behalf of someone else and their needs, knowing that our Father "is able to do immeasurably more than all we ask or imagine, according to His power that is at work within us" (Ephesians 3:20). It is our duty as disciples to pray for lost souls, whether we know them or not.

Prayers of Supplication: Praying the prayers of supplication tell God that we are depending on Him to supply all of our needs. As children of God, we should not worry about anything. We should have so much faith and trust in God that we can just turn all of our concerns over to Him in prayer. Paul said that we should be anxious for nothing, but in everything by prayer and supplication, with thanksgiving, we should let our requests be known to God (Philippians 4:6 NKJV).

Prayers of Gratitude: We pray with a grateful spirit, giving God thanks for all things. He made us and saved us from our sins. He is the provider of everything we need and some of the things we want. Because of who He is to us, we give Him thanks. Paul said that in everything we should give thanks, for this is the will of God in Christ

Jesus for you. The thanks that we give is that God is in all things (1 Thessalonians 5:18). Prayers of thanksgiving can and often do lead into praise for all of God's goodness to us.

Fasting and Praying: During prayer and fasting, the believer prayerfully seeks the Lord without indulging in food or drink. It is a spiritual discipline that enhances our relationship with God as our focus is on Him and His power and ability to answer prayers. Jesus taught that fasting and praying are in order but must be done for the right reasons. It is personal and is between God and the one who is praying (Matthew 6:16–17). The act of fasting and praying is a humbling experience. It helps us to deal with challenges and conflicts in life. It tells God that we need Him and are depending on Him to meet our needs because we do not have the power to do it ourselves.

Evangelist

As Christians, we are ambassadors for Jesus Christ. We represent Him in all that we do. We are the only hands, feet, and eyes that God has on earth today, so we must serve as God's witnesses, telling a world of dying people that Jesus saves. There are so many people who need to make life changes, from living for Satan to living for God, but do not know how to go about finding their way to Him. In the life of the Christian, evangelism is not an option; it is a requirement. Once we accept Jesus Christ as our personal Savior and learn of Him and His goodness, it becomes our responsibility to share the good news with others. It is God's desire that all people be saved. Just before Jesus ascended back to heaven, He gave a commandment to His disciples in regard to evangelizing the whole world. They were to go out and make more disciples, baptize them in the name of the Father and of the Son and of the Holy Spirit, and teach them to obey everything He commanded them to do (Matthew 28:19–20). This same principle applies to all believers today.

As disciples of God, we must be alert, prayed up, and prepared to share the Gospel at all times. Every man, woman, boy, and girl deserves to know that Jesus loves them. Not only does He love us, but He proved His love for us when He sent His Son Jesus Christ from heaven to live among humankind, preaching, teaching healing, and ultimately dying on the cross for the sins of the world. Jesus fulfilled His God-given mission when He died a horrendous death on the cross at Calvary, and He did it for us. His death made salvation, sanctification, and eternal life become a reality to all of humankind. To receive one's salvation is one of the simplest tasks on earth that a person can attain. Be mindful now that it cannot be earned in any shape, form, or fashion; nor can it be bought. It is a gift from God because He loves you. All you have to do through faith is to confess with your mouth that Jesus Christ is Lord, and believe in your heart that He died on the cross for our sins and that God raised Him from the dead, and you will be saved. It is with our hearts that we believe and are justified, and it is with our mouths that we confess and are saved (Roman 10:9–10).

Jesus was teaching how valuable every single person is to God when He told two parables of lost items and one of a person who just walked away. The first one was about a man who had one hundred sheep and one of them wandered away. The man left the ninety-nine sheep to go look for the lost one.

When he found it, he was so happy and called his friends to let them know that he had found the lost sheep. After telling the story, Jesus told them that in the same way the man rejoiced after finding the one lost sheep, there will be more rejoicing in heaven over one sinner who repents than over ninety-nine persons who do not need to repent. The second one was about a woman who lost a silver coin and rejoiced when she found it. The Bible says in the same way she rejoiced over finding her coin, there is rejoicing in the presence of the angels of God over one sinner who repents. The last one was about a young man who asked his father for his share of the estate. After receiving his wealth, he went off and squandered it. When he had nothing left and was hungry, he went back home to his father. His father was watching and waiting for his return, and when he saw him coming, he ran to him and welcomed him home. The young man apologized for his behavior, and the father showed his forgiveness by planning a feast in his honor. When his brother was unhappy about his return, his father said that his son had been dead but was now alive, had been lost and was now found. In the same way, God gives us an opportunity to repent of our sins and graciously and lovingly accepts us back into the family of God (Luke 15:2–24).

It is imperative that we get outside of the comfortable walls of our homes and the church house to spread the good news of our Lord and Savior Jesus Christ. It is true that telling the good news of Jesus Christ can be done through modern technology, but remember that not all people have access to social media. People who live in undeveloped countries, the poor, and the homeless are still in need of a Savior. Going out onto street corners to witness might seem obsolete and in some cases frightening, but it is still very much needed and is in keeping with what Jesus said in one of His parables, "Go out into the highways and hedges and compel them to come that My house may be filled" (Luke 14:23 KJV). Today, in this twenty-first century, it is still the responsibility of every Christian to go out and tell anyone and everyone the good news of Jesus Christ. People cannot believe in Jesus Christ unless they hear about Him, and they cannot hear about Him unless someone tells them. Paul said how beautiful are the feet of those who bring the good news of Jesus Christ (Romans 10:14–15).

In Mark's Gospel, he took it a step further after Jesus told the disciples to go into the world and preach the good news to all creation, and that whoever believes and is baptized will be saved; he added that whoever does not believe will be condemned (Mark 16:15–16). We cannot force salvation on anyone, as it is a gift from Father God. It is their choice to accept or reject Jesus Christ as their Savior. However, in the big scheme of things, when we evangelize, God just might be using us to plant the seed or even water it, but it is He and only He who can and will give the increase (1 Corinthians 3:5–8), so it behooves us to witness as the opportunity presents itself. God has made salvation possible for everyone. We must never assume that someone is saved or does not care to be saved. It is our duty to witness to them. Of course, we will encounter some rejections, but we must keep in mind that they are not rejecting us but Jesus Christ. So we must do as Paul told Timothy, "Keep your head in all situations, endure hardships, do the work of an evangelist" (2 Timothy 4:5).

Oftentimes during witnessing, a believer's testimony is appropriate. This testimony tells why and how they accepted Jesus Christ as Lord and Savior and the changes that have come into their life since receiving their salvation. We share what God has done and is doing in our lives since we now have a personal relationship with Him. We want them to become aware that if God saved us, He can save anybody else, and most of all, He wants them saved.

What about your discipleship?

Chapter 4

Worship

To worship is to glorify and celebrate God by giving Him sincere honor, glory, and praises that acknowledge Him for who He is. We know Him to be our Creator, our Savior, and our Sustainer. We are His, and He is ours; therefore, our worship should be directed toward Him and Him alone. We do not worship Him to get something out of it but because we know who He is and what He is to us. This is the heart of our sincere worship to Him. True worship comes from the heart and is the result of our intimate relationship with Him. Worship is not just another activity we participate in when in church; it is an integral part of our lives that is ongoing in our hearts, souls, and minds. It comes out of adoration and love for God as we live our lives according to His commands. We prepare our hearts for worship, and the Holy Spirit does the rest.

Worship brings us into the presence of the Lord, so when we worship Him, we allow ourselves to decrease and Him to increase. We celebrate and acknowledge Him for who He is to us right now, who He has been to us in the past, and who He is going to be to us in the future. A psalmist who realized who God is and what He was to him extended an invitation to the people to worship God. He wanted them to know that God is worthy of all honor and glory and that nothing should be in their hearts to prevent the worship. He called for a gathering to sing and shout aloud unto the Lord because he said, "He is the Rock of our salvation." And since He is the Rock of our salvation, he invited them to come before the Lord with thanksgiving and express their love for Him with both musical instruments and loud singing of praise. He said the Lord is a great God and is above any other thing that is called a god. He said that God has the whole world in His hands. He created it and is in control of it. Then he invited them to bow down and worship Him, the Lord their Maker, for He is God, and they are His people (Psalm 95:1–7). This invitation is applicable for us today because God is the same good and Almighty God today as He was in the days of the psalmist's writing.

Spirit of Worship

Our spirit of worship toward God depends upon our relationship with Him. We must first know who He is for ourselves, not what someone else said about Him. The spirit of worship begins in the heart of the believer. Therefore, our personal relationship with Him determines the level of worship that we can offer Him. To worship God is a privilege and not a chore. To worship Him with all our hearts and minds is a mind-set, not a plan or part of a program. We worship God for His goodness and mercy in our short, spontaneous prayers and praise, as well as the time we set aside for worship. As we put things of life in the proper perspective, we understand that He is our Shepherd and we are the sheep in need of His protection and provisions; therefore, we put no other gods (things) before Him. He is the One and only true God who is worthy of our worship. An attitude of worship is pleasing in the sight of God because it shows Him that we know that He is the provider of all things and everything. All that we have and all that we are comes from Him and only Him.

It's our spirit of worship that leads us to worship God all the time and in many ways. We worship Him during the good times as well as the bad times in our lives. Jesus said that the mouth speaks from the overflow of the heart (Luke 6:45b). We thank and praise Him for the good to let Him know that we appreciate what He has done for us. We thank Him during the bad times because we realize it could be worse. We don't rejoice over a broken arm or leg, but we thank and praise God that we did not lose the arm or leg. We don't praise Him that the car was totaled but that the driver was safe. We truly worship God when we have been disobedient to His Word, and as a result, we pray sincere prayers of repentance and know that we are forgiven. We worship Him when we sincerely give of our time, money and service. We worship Him when we study His Word to learn about Him and to love Him for who He is. Worship should be done with a joyful spirit, as the palmist wrote. He said to joyfully enter into the presence of the Lord, worship Him with gladness; come before Him with joyful songs (Psalm 100:1–2).

During our regular prayer time, humility is a very important factor. As we offer praises and thanksgivings, we are able to bow and kneel in His presence. Bowing down and kneeling before the Lord is worship all in itself. We put ourselves low to look up to the Almighty God on High, the Creator of all things. We humble ourselves in His presence, acknowledging that we are lower than He is, as He is our Creator. We realize that the creation is never greater than the Creator (Psalm 95:1–6). He deserves all the honors and praises we can give to Him.

The Lord's Day

When God gave Moses the Ten Commandments for His people to live by, He required that His people set aside one day of the week for rest and worship. He designated the last day of the week because He created the earth in six days, and He rested on the seventh day. He did not need rest, but He knew people needed to rest, so He set an example for them. In that fourth commandment, He said, "Remember the Sabbath day by keeping it holy. Six days you shall labor and do all your work, but the seventh day is a Sabbath to the Lord your God" (Exodus 20:8–10a). The Jewish people acknowledged the Sabbath day as not being optional but a requirement by the Lord, as God had declared a penalty of death for those who did not obey the commandment. The Sabbath is a holy day, and it is a sign that Israel knew the Lord and how He had blessed them.

The first Christians, who were Jewish, continued attending the temple and synagogues for worship and instruction in the scriptures along with the other Jewish people. But because of their belief in Jesus Christ as the Messiah, uneasiness developed among them, and they separated themselves from the temple and synagogues. They then went into private homes for their worship services. They no longer acknowledged the last day of the week as their Sabbath but instead acknowledged the first day of the week as the Lord's Day to show reverence to God and to rest, because this was the day of Jesus' resurrection from the dead. On Sunday, the Lord's Day, Christians set aside this time to honor God and to rest. Because it is customary to begin Sundays with worship services, Christians all over the world gather with other believers to worship God and celebrate His love for us. Christians attend churches, worship centers, and other places for worship as a sign of faith and trust in God and to seek to have a closer relationship with Him. Sunday is a holy day for us. We acknowledge God's goodness and mercy by making Him more important than anything else we do on this day.

Daily Living

Our daily living is the truest form of worship to God. It comes from the heart and out of our love and obedience to Him. How we live daily is a true picture of our obedience to the teachings of Jesus Christ. This world has a set of standards for its people that are opposite of the moral standards God has set for His people. There is a visible difference in the way Christians interact with others compared to the way the people of the world interact with one another. When we were of the world, we did the same kind of unholy things the people of the world are doing today. Being new creatures in Christ and being transformed by the renewing of our minds, we do not do and say the unholy thing we used to do and say. Nor do we go to the same places we used to go. God wants us to be holy, as He is holy, and we demonstrate this by honoring Him with our living as we come in contact with people every day.

To act religious is not enough for God. He wants His people to be real in their worship. When people profess to honor and worship Him, but their hearts are not into the worship, Jesus says of them, "These people honor me with their lips, but their hearts are far from me; they worship me in vain" (Matthew 15:8–9a). This kind of worship is mere lip service and is empty. God does not want superficial worship but, instead, sincere worship from the heart as we give Him time and space in our lives. Not only do we worship in our hearts, but our worship is physical as well. We must always be aware of those around us who might need help or who could use an encouraging word, and we must offer prayers for those we encounter daily. Therefore, we worship God by our words, our thoughts, and our deeds. Without thinking about it, in our hearts, we are able to enter joyfully into His presence with an attitude of praise. Worshiping God with our daily living is a part of us. It is who we are and what we do. It represents who we are in Christ Jesus. These are some aspects of daily living that come from the heart and soul. Sometimes they are planned, and sometimes they happen spontaneously. Whatever the case might be, they are a part of our daily living as the Spirit of God lives in us.

Continuous Prayer and Praise

Continuous prayer and praise to God is an ongoing endeavor in the life of the Christian. It's a lifestyle. It can be done anywhere and at any time since God is omnipresent and omniscience. Our hearts lead us to praise God at all times because He is worthy of being praised. One of the highest commendations Christians can give to God is through praise and worship. Moses said to the Jewish people, "He is your praise, He is your God, who performed for you those great and awesome wonders you saw with your own eyes" (Deuteronomy 10:21). This holds true for us today, as God is still blessing us every day of our lives, starting with waking us up from our sleep every morning. As we assess our lives daily, we think of His goodness to us, and we give Him the honor and heartfelt praises that are due Him. This can be done in church, at home, driving, during your lunch hour at work, or really any place you might be. Our continuous prayers and praise of thanksgiving are a part of us as we thank Him for the goodness, grace, and mercy He bestows upon us every day of our lives.

When we praise God, we express our joy to Him for all He is to us. Praise and joy go hand in hand because one cannot praise God and be sad. The psalmist wrote that it is good to sing praises to our God because it is pleasant and beautiful (Psalm 147:1). As we express praises to God, we empty ourselves with heartfelt expressions of joy to Him for His love, goodness, and mercy. It comes from deep within as we honor and celebrate His love for us. We identify with the psalmist who gives good reasons for us to always praise and worship God. He wrote that God is our helper, our keeper, and our protector. He watches over us day and night. He will preserve and protect us from all evil. He preserves our souls and preserves our going in and coming out (Psalm 121:1– 8).

One psalmist believed that God deserves praise and honor from all that He created. He wrote that not only should people praise God but that all of His creations should praise Him. The question is, how do all of God's creations praise Him? He says they praise Him when they do what He created them to do, so that the heavens and the earth can function properly. After his call for the other creations to praise God, he called for the rulers of all nations and young men, young women, old men and women, and children to praise Him because His name alone is exalted, and His splendor is above the earth and the heavens (Psalm 148:1–13). If God expects all of His other creations to praise Him, surely humankind, the highest level of His creations, created in His image, should praise Him.

Prayers are personal and can be done verbally or silently, individually or collectively. Wherever we are, we can thank God for His goodness. We give Him thanks for all things—not only for meeting our basic needs but for the sunshine and the rain and the air we breathe. We thank and praise Him for who we are and for our accomplishments, because without Him, we are nothing. But most of all, we thank Him for our salvation. We thank Him for allowing His only begotten Son, Jesus Christ, to die on the cross for the sins of the world. We thank and praise Him for the Holy Spirit who lives in us to lead and guide us in God's holy way, and we thank Him for His holy Word, the road map to heaven. Our acknowledgment of His goodness does not come to an end until we thank Him for providing us the opportunity to spend eternal life with Him.

Yes, church is the place designated to worship God on Sunday morning, along with prayer meeting and Bible study on Wednesday nights, but it does not stop there. God can be worshiped anytime and anywhere. Praising God should be a seven-day-of-the-week endeavor for the believer. There should always be a song in our hearts and praises on our lips. Our prayerful and praising spirit prompts us to praise Him no matter where we are. In our hearts, we can joyfully enter into His presence with an attitude of praise. Depending upon where we are, our worship can be soft or even silent. Other times, it can be loud and joyful. Throughout the day and night, we take advantage of every opportunity to offer praises and thanksgiving in our hearts for all things.

We also praise God through singing songs of praise. Praise songs are expressions of love and gratitude to God. They can be songs in the heart for self-fulfillment or songs sung openly for others to enjoy. Singing songs of praise to God can have positive effects on our spirits. They can be uplifting and give peace of mind. The lyrics proclaim God's greatness by giving Him credit for what He has done. Songs of praise indicate that we realize

He is all we need and we are grateful that we have a relationship with Him. They are our reactions to God for His greatness. They remind us of His faithfulness. Many artists write and sing songs of praise to God as a result of victories they have achieved, accomplishments and trials and tribulations in their personal lives that God has seen them through.

Music and singing are important aspects of churches and worship centers all over the world. Music adds to the worship service in a special kind of heartfelt way. It helps to lead a person's thoughts and emotions to God as He is praised for all His goodness. Music was created by God in order that it be used to worship and praise Him. In the Old Testament, King David instituted music in the temple services (1 Chronicles 16:4–7), and it became a very important part of their worship services. The psalmist wrote to praise God for His greatness with the sounding of the trumpet, the harp and lyre, the tambourine, strings and flute, with the clash of cymbals and with dancing (Psalm 150:2–5).

The singing of songs played a very important part in the early church services. Paul admonished the early Christians to sing and make music in their hearts to the Lord, and to always give thanks to Him for everything (Ephesians 5:19-20). Dance and drama are other means of praising God. In Bible days, the psalmist wrote to praise God's name with dancing and to make music for Him with tambourines and harps (Psalm 149:3). Dancing before the Lord is not a new way to worship Him. King David, dressed in a linen ephod, danced before the Lord in his reaction to the ark being brought back home to Jerusalem after a brief Palestine captivity (2 Samuel 6:14). Many churches today have praise and worship dance teams that perform to honor God and His goodness.

Zadia B. Tyson

Diligent Study of Scriptures

The purpose of studying scriptures is to gain wisdom, understanding, and knowledge and to have joy in the Lord. Everything we need to know or do in this life is in the Bible. God's Word is the light we need to show us the way from walking in the darkness of this world. The psalmist wrote that God's Word is a light unto his feet and a light to his path (Psalm 119:105). With God's Word as our guide, we, like the psalmist, will not walk in darkness. Studying scriptures provides spiritual nourishment for the soul. We need spiritual food for the soul just as we need physical food for our bodies. Jesus said that man does not live on bread alone but from every word that comes from the mouth of God (Matthew 4:4).

Scriptures are the inspired Word of God; therefore, everything taught in the church should be scriptural and not of humankind. God inspired prophets and apostles to write them, but they originated with Him. The Bible says no prophecy of scripture came about by the prophet's own interpretation and that men spoke through God as they were carried along by the Holy Spirit (2 Peter 1:20–21). The apostle Paul wrote, "All Scripture is given by the inspiration of God and, and is profitable for doctrine, for reproof, for correction, for instruction in righteousness" (2 Timothy 3:16 NKJV). Scriptures are not just words but are standards set by God for His people. They are designed for us to live moral and upright lifestyles. The Bible gives us instructions and hope. It helps us to grow in the Christian faith as we learn the truth about God, what He wants us to know, and what He wants us to do. The Word of God is powerful, as it is life changing. As we study the Word, we find out who and what we are. The writer of Hebrews said, "God's Word is living and active. It is sharper than any double-edged sword. It penetrates to divide our soul and spirit, joints and marrow; it judges the thoughts and attitudes of the heart" (Hebrews 4:12).

God inspired the prophets and apostles to write the Bible to direct us to the path of salvation, sanctification, and finally eternal life. The Bible says that we are to let the Word of God live in us richly as we teach and admonish one another with wisdom, and as we sing spiritual songs with gratitude to God (Colossians 3:16). It is the Word of God that leads people to faith in Jesus Christ. It reveals the love God has for humankind, and we learn to honor Him. It teaches us how to live holy and righteous lives in a corrupt world. It reveals the true nature of Satan, God's enemy, and his purpose here on earth. Knowing and obeying God's Word is an effective weapon against temptations. Jesus used scriptures to counteract Satan's attacks when He was without food for forty days and was hungry (Luke 4:1–13). He was successful in doing so, and when we know God's Word, through the power of the Holy Spirit that lives in us, we can too.

Memorizing scriptures is good, but it does not stop us from sinning. We must allow the Word of God to penetrate our hearts so that we can apply it to our daily living, which will help us to recognize sin and rebuke it. One psalmist wrote, "I have hidden your word in my heart so that I might not sin against thee" (Psalm 119:11). Christians diligently study God's Word because we are driven to do so. We have to put in quality time studying it so we will understand what God's plans are for our lives. The Word teaches us that, as Christians, we are going to have our share of trials and tribulations. It is a misconception on our part to think that because we are Christians, everything in our lives will be peaches and cream; however, the Word does teach us that no matter what we are going through, God is with us. The apostle Paul said that we should be diligent to present ourselves approved to God, workers who does not need to be ashamed, rightly dividing the word of truth (2 Timothy 2:15 NKJV).

Someone came up with the acronym BIBLE: basic instructions before leaving earth.

God's Word is given to us so that we can know His will and way for our lives. He wants us to know His truth, speak it, and apply it to our daily living. Not only is it imperative that we know the Word of God, but it is even more imperative that we obey it.

Obedience to God's Word

Obedience to God's Word reveals our faith and trust in Him and is based on our love for Him. Jesus said to His disciples, "If you love me, you will obey what I command" (John 14:15, 21). God does not force us to obey Him but gives us choices and leaves it up to us as to whether we will obey Him or disobey Him. Obedience to God begins with humility. We have to know in our hearts that His way is better than ours could ever be. It is not enough to say we believe what is right; we must do what we know is right according to God's Word, even when we do not understand it. The Bible says that we should not merely listen to the Word and deceive ourselves, but we must do what it says. Anyone who listens to the Word and does not obey it is like a man who looks at his face in a mirror, and after looking at himself, he goes away and immediately forgets what he looks like. The man who looks intently at the Word and continues to do so will not forget what he has heard but will practice it (James 1:22–25).

Knowing scriptures but not living in obedience to them is like not knowing them at all. We can't be the disciples God has called us to be if we cannot or do not obey His Word. Obeying

God's Word makes it easier to obey the rules and regulations of our land. Obedience to God's commands cannot be negotiated. Whenever there is a situation where we have to make a choice to obey God or humankind, we must obey God. Everything that He commands us to do is for our spiritual health. There is life and eternal life when we live in obedience to God's Word. To live apart from His Word is spiritual death.

Not only does God command that we obey Him, but when we do, He rewards us for our obedience. Among many other things, obedience leads to peace with God and with others. Knowing and obeying God's Word is an effective weapon against temptation. Jesus used scriptures to counter Satan's attacks, and we can too (Luke 4:1–13). God expects us to be walking in obedience to His will and way when we come to Him with our requests. When we obey His commands and do what pleases Him, we can receive anything we ask of Him (John 15:7). John also said that the person who says, "I know God," but does not do what He commands is a liar (1 John 2:4).

Spirit of Forgiveness

A spirit of forgiveness is a Christian virtue. We are required to forgive; it is not an option. As Christians, we must make that important decision to let go of anger and resentment for any wrong that has been committed toward us. It can be difficult sometimes, but God requires us to forgive, and the Holy Spirit living in us makes it possible. He requires us to forgive others because He forgave us for our sins. Once we can forgive ourselves as God has forgiven us, we can forgive others. God is the supreme forgiver of sin. He forgives us, His people, time and again for our sins as we approach Him for forgiveness. Because He forgives us, we too must forgive others time and again, without counting. It is so important to God that we forgive our brothers and sisters that Jesus said if we forgive those who sin against us, our Father in heaven will forgive us of our sins. He added that if we do not forgive, our Father in heaven will not forgive us of our sins (Matthew 6:14–15).

The apostle Paul said that we must be kind to one another, tenderhearted, forgiving one another as God has forgiven us (Ephesians 4:32). We should address all sinful acts toward us and quickly forgive the one who committed the wrong against us. Jesus taught His disciples how to practice forgiveness. He said when we are wronged by someone; we are to call it to their attention. Calling it to their attention must be done in love and with the intent to forgive, because it is our duty to help each other. True, sincere forgiveness has no limitations. When and if people who wronged us ask for forgiveness, we must forgive them as many times as they ask. We might feel hurt inside, and we may want to hold a grudge, but instead, we are to forgive over and over and not keep score of the offenses. Jesus said that if your brother sins against you seven times in a day and comes back to you seven times asking for forgiveness, you must forgive him (Luke 17:4). Forgiveness frees us because even if the offender does not ask you for forgiveness, you are now free to receive God's forgiveness.

Give Back to God

The Bible is very clear about the importance of giving in the life of the Christian. Christians should see giving as an opportunity to bless someone who is in need. It is an act of worship when we share with others what God has given to us. We show love when we are able to give without reservation. Our giving should come from the heart. We should first give to God by spending time with Him daily in the Word and prayers of gratitude. Our giving should also honor God; we do this when we give to the poor and meet the immediate needs of others. God blesses those who give to the poor; he said they would not go lacking. He instructed Solomon to write that he who gives to the poor lends to the Lord, and God Himself will pay back what he has given (Proverbs 19:17, 28:27).

Our giving should never be about the amount we give or the amount of time we spend doing something for someone, but more about how we give it or do it. Our attitude plays a very important part in our giving. It should be sincere and pure, without any ulterior motives. God knows our hearts, and He knows what we have. Sincere giving honors God and His Word. Scriptures teach that when we give, it should be done generously and that each person should give what they decide upon in their heart to give. The giver should not give reluctantly or under compulsion, because God loves a cheerful giver (2 Corinthians 9:7).

In one segment of Jesus' first sermon (the Sermon on the Mount), He taught about giving to the needy. He condemned the practice of showing off one's giving just to impress others. He said that our charitable deeds should be done in secret and not before others to be seen by them. God knows what you have done, and He Himself will reward you openly for giving (Matthew 6:1–4 NKJV). We should never be concerned with not having enough for ourselves after giving. God has more than enough for all of us. We sing a song at church that says, "You can't beat God giving. The more you give, the more He gives to you." The Bible verifies this in Luke 6:38: Jesus said to give, and it will be given back to us. Whatever we give, we will receive back in full measure. The Bible teaches that our giving can come back to us a hundredfold (Mark 10:29–30). That should not be the reason for our giving, but instead because we love the Lord and want to be in obedience to His Word. When we give to help others, we are blessing the Lord.

Faithful Church Attendance

Faithful church attendance is important in the life of the Christian. Jesus set the perfect example for us by attending services in the synagogues. He was the Son of God, yet He went to the synagogue on a regular basis to be in and participate in the services (Luke 4:16). It is very important for us as Christians to meet and assemble with those who have the same spiritual beliefs we have. The author of the book of Hebrews said that believers should not give up meeting together, because this is an ideal time to encourage one another in the Lord (Hebrews 10:25). As we come together, we worship God together by reading and hearing His Word, rendering our service according to the gifts God has given us, giving of our tithes and offerings, singing songs of Zion, and fellowshipping with our brothers and sisters in Christ.

Not only do we attend church faithfully on Sunday morning, but we also are faithful in our attendance to Sunday school, Bible study, prayer meetings, and other spiritual gatherings to worship and praise God. Attending these types of services indicate that we have a desire for a stronger personal relationship with our Lord and Savior. We learn more about Him and have the opportunity to encourage others with our testimonies.

Partake of the Lord's Supper

The Lord's Supper, or Communion, began with Jesus Christ as He had His final meal with His beloved disciples. It was at this meal that He told them of His sacrificial death. The Lord's Supper or communion is the partaking of bread and wine by the believer, as a continuous memorial of the broken body and the shed blood of Jesus Christ. It is a celebration of the death of our Lord and Savior Jesus Christ. When we partake of it, it allows us, as Christians, to reflect on what God did for us when He allowed His beloved Son to die on the cross for the sins of the world so that we could have eternal life.

Jesus instituted the first Lord's Supper while He and His disciples were eating the Passover meal together. While reclined at a table with them, He told them that He desired to eat that Passover meal with them before He suffered. He used bread, which represented His body, and a cup of wine that represented His blood as He offered Himself as a sacrifice. "He took the bread, gave thanks, broke it, and gave it to His disciples saying, 'Take it, this is my body given for you; do this in remembrance of Me.' Then He took the cup, gave thanks and offered it to them saying, 'Drink from it, all of you. This is my blood of the covenant which is poured out for many for the forgiveness of sins'" (Matthew 26:26–28; Luke 22:14–20).

As Christians, we believe that Communion is one of the ordinances Jesus instituted for the church to observe until He returns. He told us to do this in remembrance of Him. He did not say how often the church should participate in this memorial but that we should do it. We believe that it is more important to participate in it with the right spirit, rather than the focus being on the number of times we partake in it. As we eat the bread and drink the wine, we are to remember Jesus' faithfulness when He came to earth to fulfill His God-given mission, which was to save people from their sins.

What about your worship?

Chapter 5

Fellowship

Christian fellowship begins with God in the heart of the believer. Our fellowship with Him is through our prayers, our praise through worship, our discipleship, and our stewardship. Not only do we as Christians fellowship with God the Father, but scriptures says we fellowship with Jesus Christ, the Holy Spirit, and with other believers as well (1 John 1:3, 7; 1 Corinthians 1:9). Being in the family of God enhances fellowship among the believers because God is our Father. Christian fellowship is based on relationships that develop as people interact with one another. The basis for fellowship among believers is love as we open up our hearts to fellow believers. It is about living in peace and harmony with each other, showing sympathy, compassion, and humility. We gain strength from this bond that has formed as we fellowship with one another. Fellowshipping with one another becomes a beneficial experience for all involved because of what and who we have in common. The nature of fellowshipping with other Christians helps us to stay anchored in Jesus Christ and His teachings.

The new converts in the first church in Jerusalem realized the importance of fellowshipping. They stressed the sharing of spiritual things. The Bible says they devoted themselves to the apostles' teaching, to fellowship, to the breaking of bread, and to prayer. All the believers were together and had everything in common. They sold their possessions in order to share with those who did not have. They continued to meet every day in the temple courts until they could not meet there anymore because of their belief in Jesus Christ. So they started to meet in individual homes for communion, meals, praising God with sincere hearts, and enjoying the company of all the people (Acts 2:42–47). It is through fellowship that God's love shines through us as we interact with each other. It is showing one another that we care about what they care about; that we hurt when they hurt; that we rejoice when they rejoice. It allows us to share our love, our joy, our disappointments, and our pain. Fellowshipping gives us the strength to endure our trials and tribulations as we share the love of God.

Christian fellowship means there is a positive relationship between people having the same interests, as in the early church. Traveling evangelists went from town to town to help establish new churches. One man named Gaius welcomed them into his home and provided food and lodging, as those missionaries depended on the hospitality of fellow believers in the towns they stopped in (3 John 1:5–6). Our fellowship today is somewhat different from that of the early church in this area, but the purpose is basically the same. Today evangelists are housed in hotels along with other amenities. The focus on sharing and caring for each other remains the same. The author of the book of Hebrews tells us that we should consider one another in order to stir up love and good works (Hebrews 10:24 NKJV). This is usually done in the various ministries of the church, such as in prayer meetings, mission groups, and brotherhood and women's ministry, and oftentimes over refreshments. We support the church's benevolent ministry, where love offerings are given to those who are in distress or have emergency needs. Foreign mission is also a part of the church's plan for sharing and caring. Christian fellowship is still about sharing and caring but on another level. We will probably never see any of the people who receive our financial support, but we care and share because that's the Christian's way. Christian fellowship builds Christian relationships.

Relationships

The most important relationship we can have is with our Lord and Savior Jesus Christ. God the Father is everything to us. He loves, blesses, protects, and provides for us. We depend on Him for everything. We acknowledge Him as Lord by worshiping Him, praying to Him, and blessing others. As Christians, our relationship with others must be an offspring of our relationship with Jesus Christ. We live in communities of believers as well as nonbelievers, and we interact with all of them on a daily basis. Some of the nonbelievers are members of our families, others are old friends, and some are coworkers. We have good relationships with them, but it is impossible for us to have Christian fellowship with them; therefore, we must know our limits of associating with them. We cannot completely stay away from them because of who they are to us. But we must avoid certain kinds of entertainment with them that leads to sin. We associate with them, but we don't! We must create an atmosphere that enhances peace and harmony among everyone. The apostle Paul said that Christians should not be yoked together with unbelievers, meaning we should not share in the unbeliever's lifestyle. He made his point by asking, "What do righteousness and wickedness have in common? Or what fellowship can light have with darkness?" Then he said, "What does a believer have in common with an unbeliever?" Yes, Paul said that we should come out from among them and be separate; he is telling us to stay close to God so we can carry out His will for our lives without distractions (2 Corinthians 6:14-17a).

It is the duty of the Christian to love everybody, and we cannot show love without interaction. Therefore, it is important that we not isolate ourselves from the unsaved population of the world. If we did that, we would put ourselves in the position of not being able to share the good news of Jesus Christ with them. Jesus told His disciples to go out into the world and preach the good news about Him to everyone. This message still applies to us today. We don't need to preach it to the saved persons but to the unsaved ones.

Humility

As Christians, we must have a humble spirit because humility is of God. In our humility, we are able to see ourselves for who we are from God's perspective and act accordingly. We are only who He made us to be. Paul said that we ought not to think more highly of ourselves than we should; instead, we should think of ourselves with sober judgment in accordance with the measure of faith given to us by God (Roman 12:3). We are no more than God has allowed us to be and have no more than He blessed us to have. We understand our limitations and acknowledge the fact that it is only through the Holy Spirit that we can do any good thing. We live every day knowing that our accomplishments are not of us but of God and that we can do all things through Christ, who gives us the strength (Philippians 4:13).

It is in our humble state that we bring honor to God for who He is and to others as well. Because of who we are in Christ Jesus, the apostle Paul said that we should be imitating His humility. He said that we should do nothing out of selfish ambition or vain conceit, but in humility, we should consider others better than ourselves and look not to our own interests but to the interests of others (Philippians 2:3-5). The acronym JOY in the life of the Christian has been around for a long time: if you want joy in your life, you must put *Jesus* first, *others* next, and *yourself* last." This is a true picture of humility in the life of the believer!

Sincerity

To be sincere is to be without deceit or pretense. Paul wrote that there is a blessing for those who love our Lord Jesus Christ in sincerity (Ephesians 6:24 NKJV). Being real with God is an absolute necessity, as He knows all about us and our ways and thoughts. Being sincere in our relationship with God will extend into sincerity in our relationships with others. Transparency is a necessity in all relationships. It must be obvious that our actions and attitudes do not have ulterior motives. We must be who we say we are and do what we say we will do, without any false pretenses or hidden agendas. Sincerity in relationships indicates integrity, humility, and love. Honesty is always the best policy, as it is a Christian virtue.

Encourage

It is because of the Holy Spirit that lives in us that we are prompted to encourage, inspire, and help one another. Scriptures teach that we should encourage one another and build each other up (1 Thessalonians 5:11). Christians are called to be encouragers, and we must take advantage of every opportunity that presents itself to offer words of encouragement, comfort, consolation, and counsel to help someone who is in a crisis. Encouraging words can help change the lives of those who appear to feel worthless, helpless, and hopeless. This change can come as a result of some simple encouraging words or even a smile with a greeting. No person is an island, meaning we don't live alone, without having to come in contact with other people. God gave us families, friends, coworkers, and so many more people in our lives for a reason. It is very important that people know that someone cares about them as a person, and one way to show it is through words of encouragement and actions. As Christians, we should offer encouraging words to anyone we come in contact with who needs it, not just brothers and sisters in Christ. The unsaved person too can be lifted up when encouraged. This might be a prime opportunity to tell them about the love of God.

Good Listener

There will be times when we should do more listening than talking. Sometimes people just need to empty themselves to someone who will listen without judging and without interrupting. It is during these times when they have a listening ear that they can feel free to share their struggles and temptations. A good listener is an asset to any group assembled for fellowship, as well as in a one-on-one situation. When we have the opportunity to speak, the apostle Paul said our conversation should be full of grace and seasoned with salt, so that we may know how to answer everyone. This means that we must be courteous and respectful and give meaningful words of encouragement (Colossians 4:6). If we are interacting with unsaved people, this might very well be the opportunity to give our testimony of what God has done for us. This might also be the ideal time to witness to them about how much God loves them and wants them to be saved from their sins.

What about your fellowship?

Chapter 6

Stewardship

Christian stewardship refers to the responsibility that Christians have to maintain and use wisely the gifts that God has given to us. It is the act of taking care of something that does not belong to us but to God. God is the Creator of the world and all that is in it; consequently, He is the owner of all things. Therefore, everything we have comes from the Lord. He gives it to us for us to use, enjoy, and share with others. When He gives something to us, He makes us stewards over it and holds us accountable for what we do with it. Everything we have accumulated, have been given or will ever have belongs to the Lord. He just made us stewards over it. Every gift and talent we have has been given to us by God, and each is to be used to glorify Him, edify the church, and serve others.

Giving and sharing are important in the life of the Christian, and it starts with us being able to give of ourselves to God first. We give to Him when we serve and bless others and spend time with Him in prayer and praise. Every time we give sincerely, it is an expression of our gratitude, love and obedience. The more God gives to us, the more He expects us to give. Jesus said, "From everyone who has been given much, much will be demanded; and from the one who has been entrusted with much, much more will be asked" (Luke 12:48b). So why are we to give, what do we give, and who do we give it to? We are to give because God has commanded us to do so. When He blesses us with something, He expects us to bless someone else. And we are to give of our resources, talents, and time, as they all come from the Lord.

The concept of stewardship began in the Old Testament. God has always expected His people to give back to Him a portion of what He has given to them. He gave Moses principles and guidelines for His people to give back to Him for the house of worship. The Israelites were to bring Him an offering so that they could make Him a sanctuary, so that He could dwell among them. He specified that the offerings were to be given willingly and from the heart of those who gave. He wanted gold, silver, bronze, specified colors of yarn, linen, skins, wood, and other high-quality materials for the tabernacle and the furniture He was going to instruct them to build (Exodus 25:1–9 NKJV).

In God's commandments for holy living, He told Moses to tell the people to bring a tithe of everything from the land, whether it be grain from the soil or fruit from the trees, or from the herd and flock. It all belongs to the Lord, as it is holy to Him (Leviticus 27:30-32). As the Israelites were about to enter the Promised Land, God gave instructions for other offerings they were to give to Him. These offerings were to teach them how to have proper fellowship with Him. The five major offerings were:

Burnt Offering: This offering was done voluntarily, and its purpose was to make payment for sins in general (Leviticus 1).

Grain Offering: This offering was done voluntarily, and its purpose was to show honor and respect to God in worship (Leviticus 2).

Fellowship Offering: This offering was done voluntarily, and its purpose was to express gratitude to God (Leviticus 3).

Sin Offering: This offering was a requirement by God, and its purpose was to make payment for unintentional sins of uncleanness, neglect, or thoughtlessness (Leviticus 4).

Guilt Offering: This offering was required by God, and its purpose was to make payment for sins against God and others. A sacrifice was made to God, and the injured person was repaid or compensated (Leviticus 5).

When God's people were disobedient to Him by not giving tithes and offerings, He addressed the issue by telling Malachi to tell them to return unto Him, and He would return to them. They wanted to know how to return to Him. He said, "Will a man rob God? Yet you rob Me! Then you ask the question, how do we rob you?" He answered, "In tithes and offerings." He added that they were under a curse because of their robbing Him. Then the Lord told them to bring the whole tithe into the storehouse, that there may be food in His house. He said, "Test Me in this, and see if I will not throw open the floodgates of heaven and pour out so much blessing that you will not have room enough for it" (Malachi 3:7–10). According to scripture, when we refuse to give back a part of what God has given to us, we rob Him. Just as God demanded that His people in the Old Testament days give back to Him in sacrifices and give to the poor, we too are to give. He expects us, His people, to give back a portion of what He has given us for the church and to help the poor, who He said will be with us always. When we give to those in need, we give back to God, who is the giver of all things.

During Jesus' Sermon on the Mount, He taught about giving to the poor. He taught His disciples two important facts. First, He said that what we give to them should not be publicized, like the hypocrites did to be honored by others. They did good deeds only to be seen, not out of compassion for the needy. Next, He said that when you give to the needy, do not let your left hand know what your right hand is doing, meaning that our motive for giving must be pure and from the heart. To be sure that your motives are pure, your giving should be done in secret, where no one knows about it but you and God. God promises to reward us for our good deeds. We don't give to be rewarded but to be obedient to God's Word (Matthew 6:1–4).

Giving is an expression of the love we have for God. When we give, God gives back to us in His own way so that we can continue to give. As members of our local churches, we give of our finances through tithes and offerings. We give our time and talents in order to serve God and so that the church will thrive. But our giving should not stop there. God created us to do good works. There are many opportunities to give back to the community and on the state and national levels. There are needy people all over the world. God does not expect us to give what we do not have, but He does expect us to give of what He has given to us. One way to show how much we love and want to obey Him is through our stewardship. When we make giving back to God our focus, the Holy Spirit will lead and guide us as to how to use our money, our talents, and our time. This way, the church can make the impact on the world as God intended it to.

Treasure

Giving of our finances is only one facet of our stewardship to God. As Christians, we should make sharing of our God-given gifts a top priority of giving back to Him, not just giving of what we have left over after using most of it for ourselves. When we truly understand the principles of stewardship, we give joyfully, knowing that our giving will not make us poor but that we are honoring God and helping to meet the needs of those who are in need. It is important that we give financially to the church because it makes it possible for the church to meet its financial obligations and carry out its God-given mission. God wants us to give as much as we are able to give, and to give it willingly, according to our means. God loves a cheerful giver. Paul said that if the willingness is there, the gift is acceptable according to what one has, not according to what one does not have (2 Corinthians 8:12). You cannot give what you do not have, but you should give of what you have.

Jesus was in the temple where the treasury was, and He had an opportunity to observe the people giving. He was not interested in how much they were giving but how they gave. He noticed that the rich people put large amounts into the treasury, but His attention was turned to a certain poor widow who put her only two coins into the treasury. Jesus called His disciples unto Him and pointed out the widow's offering. She had given all that she had to live on, and as far as she knew, no one knew what she was giving. She gave from her heart. He said that the poor widow had put in more than the others because they gave from their wealth, but she gave out of her poverty because she put in all she had to live on (Mark 12:41–44). Gifts of any size are pleasing to God when they are given with a proper attitude. Jesus encouraged giving and with a promise when He said, "Give, and it will be given back to you. A good measure, pressed down, shaken together and running over, will be poured into your lap. For with the measure you use, it will be measured to you" (Luke 6:38).

The apostle Paul taught that God does not value a gift by its size but by the attitude of the heart of the person who is giving. So the question becomes, how much should we give? Some of us believe in tithing 10 percent of our income, as God commanded of His people in the Old Testament days. Others believe that the 10 percent was applicable for Bible days only and that we should be giving more than a mere 10 percent of our income. There is another group that has reasons for giving less and has justifications for doing so. Jesus gave us instructions on how to properly handle our finances when He told the parable of the rich fool. He said that this rich man produced a good crop but had no place to store it. So he thought that he would tear down his old barns and build bigger ones to store his grains and goods. He thought he could take life easy by eating, drinking, and being merry because he had enough goods stored up to last him for many years. God called him a fool and told him that he would die that very night. He asked, "Then who will get what you prepared for yourself?" Then Jesus told the listeners that this is how it will be with anyone who stores up things for himself but is not rich toward God (Luke 12:16–21). Money is important and is needed in the world today, but money and possessions will one day pass away. All that will last are the treasures we store up in heaven.

Paul knew the importance of giving of our finances to support the church. In his second letter to the Corinthian church, he gave several principles to follow to support the church financially. First, he told them that if the willingness to give is there, their gift is acceptable according to what they have, not according to what they do not have (8:12). Secondly, he reminded them that whoever sows sparingly will also reap sparingly, and whoever sows generously will also reap generously. Then he said that each man should give what he has decided in his heart to give, and it should not be given reluctantly or under compulsion because God loves a cheerful giver (9: 6–7).

Talent

Talents are special God-given abilities. They are to be used to honor and glorify Him by blessing and serving others. All of us have at least one talent, and some people are blessed to have more than one. Whatever talents God has given to us, He expects us to use them. They are not meant to be for self-glory but to bless others. Many people are born with God-given talents. These God-given talents are meant to be used to glorify God and to enhance the lives of others. Gifts are also given to every person who accepts Jesus Christ as their Lord and Savior. They too are meant to glorify God and to edify the church. The apostle Peter said we should use whatever gift God has given us to serve others (1 Peter 4:10). Using our talents or gifts faithfully is a part of our stewardship responsibility.

Time

God created time and made it an intricate part of the lives of people, and it is controlled by Him. He has a plan for the life of every person, starting before birth. When the proper time comes, we become aware of time and should learn how to use our time wisely. God expects us to do so. He inspired King Solomon to write, "There is a time for everything and a season for every activity under heaven" (Ecclesiastes 3:1). Our first order of business is to spend time with our Father God in heaven. He appreciates the time we spend with Him in worship. Spending time with Him is priceless because we develop a closer and personal relationship with Him.

As Christians going about our daily routine of life, we must set aside quality time to be spent with God in prayer and praise and acknowledging Him as God our Creator and provider. We must also be about our Father's business of serving and blessing others. Yes, we must allow time for ourselves, but remember, in this life as a Christian, it is not about us but about Jesus Christ. God is going to hold us accountable for how we use our time. There are so many places we can spend our time helping others. The nursing homes come to mind right away because there are so many people there who have no one to come and spend time with them. Most of them are elderly, and their last days should not be dark days of loneliness and neglect.

There is so much work that needs to be done, and there are just so many hours in a day to get it done. Paul said that we should be very careful how we live and that we should take advantage of every opportunity to serve others (Ephesians 5:15). We learn early in life that we must spend our time wisely. So let us take the time to evaluate how much time we spend blessing God by blessing others. We must use our time wisely so that we can complete the necessary tasks that are set before us, because we do not know what tomorrow will bring.

What about your stewardship?

Resources

The Life Application Bible, New International Version
Tyndale House Publishers, Inc.
Wheaton, Illinois

The Holy Bible, New King James Version
Thomas Nelson Bibles, 1979

Scriptures at Your Fingertip
Howard Books
New York, NY 10020

Nelson's New Illustrated Bible Commentary
Thomas Nelson Inc., 1999

Where to Find It in the Bible
Ken Anderson
Thomas Nelson Publishers, 2001
Nashville, Tennessee

Printed in the United States
By Bookmasters